White Power and the Fade from Black

By Ceola Askew

I0408735

Foreword

In the United States, we think of race predominantly as white vs. black or strong vs. weak. While empathizing with the weak, we praise (or condemn) the strong. We think of the weak as those we must help, and we view the strong as those who can help. All of this comes from a limited and perhaps even a selfish perspective, rather than from the perspectives of those we identify as weak or strong. Strong individuals exert power – economic or physical – over the rest of us, whereas the weak are considered drains on the power source and must therefore be controlled, contained, or eliminated.

From this societal concept comes the notion of slavery. But why enslave any people? What right has one group to capture and forcefully benefit from the labor of another? It comes down not to what is right or wrong, but rather, what is fiscally beneficial and realistically manageable by the strongest group in society.

Over the past several hundred years of American history, power and money have allowed white society to become the dominant, controlling force, while weakness and poverty have led to the physical and subsequent economic enslavement of black society, even to the present time. No one wields authority like white, and no group embodies weakness as black do. The balance of social power has always been levied in favor of whites. But the time has long since come when societal equality should be balanced among all U.S. racial and ethnic groups.

INTRODUCTION

With the historical election of the first president of color, unavoidable questions beg to be answered. The most compelling one is this:

What is the current status of race relations in the United States?

The answer is just as compelling:

No change - race relations are the same as ever.

Another question rises to challenge us:

Where are race relations headed?

The answer is just as grim:

Nowhere. White-black relations are stagnant – and likely to remain that way.

Although these questions deserve valid answers, they are not as pressing as the question of how black-white relations evolved to where they are today.

The undesirable status and destination of white-black relations will never change until blacks understand their place in the relationship. No one person in a quasi-leadership role will alter the course of the black-white relationship. President Barack Obama is but one black person. While the world focuses on him as President, white America in general is focused on black history. The white part of America that voted for Obama jostles against the other half of white America screaming at his every step.

Race relations is headed nowhere and everywhere simultaneously. Whites have always had a relationship with blacks, and black America has always endured through that relationship, no matter how dysfunctional or abusive.

But with the first President of color, the black-white relationship, like a distressed marriage, has become more noticeable, more out in the open. The relationship permeates every corner of the country because of the ability of blacks and whites to live anywhere and everywhere, side by side or in separate parts of town. But the relationship is also going nowhere because there is no resulting harmony in coexistence.

For centuries it has been the same dance, different tune. When race in America is studied and chronicled, there seems to be the same omission - the history, as we know it today, has omitted the beginning. Contemporary history has committed to readily available facts; blacks were slaves; blacks were ill-treated. Whites built America; whites were ruthless and greedy. Is that the end of our shared history?

The resulting question – the overarching cry – is why?

Why were blacks used as slaves? What are the white and black differences? How did race in America get to where it is today? What is so different about one race that it can wage war on a global scale to destroy and kill with reckless abandon - and then with the stroke of a pen befriend and rebuild the enemy?

Conflict on a globe scale leads to predominantly white power.

Whites' and blacks' skin color is the obvious difference between the races. Yet, the *why* and the *how* do not get answered with just skin tones.

How could the group of former slave owners think it easy to forget the dehumanized treatment experienced by blacks' ancestors? Why are today's constant black failures always pointing to slavery? These two questions underscore the constant struggle that keeps whites on the defensive, and blacks on offense. With globalization rapidly spreading, where are whites and blacks in America going?

Blacks are both gaining and losing ground. How? There are a million black youths either in jail, getting out of jail, or dropping out of high school. An article by Sophia Kerby dated March 13, 2012, in The Center for American Progress, titled "The Top 10 Most Startling Facts About People of Color and Criminal Justice in the United States" offers dismaying statistics:

> According to the Bureau of Justice Statistics, one in three black men can expect to go to prison in their lifetime. Individuals of color have a disproportionate number of encounters with law enforcement, indicating that racial profiling continues to be a problem. A report by the Department of Justice found that blacks and Hispanics were approximately three times more likely to be searched during a traffic stop than white motorists. African Americans were twice as likely to be arrested and almost four times as likely to experience the use of force during encounters with the police.

Whites are importing able-bodied workers and shipping work out to overseas workers. This means a significant portion of the black population in the not-too-distant future will become career inmates. Some will be relegated to a hybrid third-race status of "po' black" behind Hispanics, Asians, and Middle Easterners. With Middle East soldiers returning home, there will be an influx of refugees along with veterans who will be competing for American jobs.

Blacks have problems getting in the white door, just being black. Add to that a criminal record and pair that with a GED, or small college education, and then put that up against an Iraqi that speaks two or more languages and displays an Old World work ethic - it not too hard to see that, worst case scenario, some blacks will have to go back to jail or to the back of the welfare line.

However, blacks are gaining as well. When U.S. sports teams, especially college sports and professional sports, opened their playing fields to non-Caucasians, blacks excelled. They now earn and lose astronomical sums. Some did better than others, but sports provided a venue that led to the closing of the racial financial gap. This closing is still being felt today, but not always in a constructive way. Although some blacks share their winnings with whites, as with those they marry or go into business with, or lawyers paid to keep them out of jail and accountants hired to make good use of the money provided by black bodies, or with the service industries, they still all too often miss out on other opportunities automatically enjoyed by whites, including investment opportunities and higher-level social status by those who continue to discriminate.

For the most part, blacks share their wealth with other blacks. As times change, so does black earning potential. For example, some rappers are also label owners, clothing designers, and real estate moguls. The black woman employs others to care for her children instead of sitting at home waiting on the government. Black are using all their talents, some good, some maybe questionable, to make a way for themselves. Whites are readily dating blacks; the taboo is still there, but the true color of racism in today's race relation is green, at least to a point, as some still value color over money. Just ask the former President.

*****

So where are blacks in America going? As for leaving America, no! It is the only land they have known it is the soil their ancestors worked. It is the land that tells their story in back-breaking and soul-splitting labor. They have earned the privilege of enjoying the fruits of the labors of others in America. As for the black community that gave this country Dr. Martin Luther King, those blacks are fading away. Black life in America has been documented with the same omission, the same admission, as always. Their history is known, but not fully understood. The future of race in America has always been fickle - cold and hot by turns.

American blacks have seen their rise and their decline with the rise and fall of this nation's breathing in and out of one era after another. Contemporary blacks have erased their originality with tattoos, piercings, dieting in excess, the mixing of races, abandoning education, and forgetting their past. Black will soon be just a color in the crayon box. The black man will be viewed in wax museums and history books as a forgotten and forsaken figure left behind in the wake of times past.

While black skin color was either brown, dark brown, or tannish with purple tones, blacks were never truly black. Blacks were taught to embrace the term *black*. Being black meant something in terms of culture and identity. What it did not mean was to be devoid of color; it meant to carry oneself with an understated attitude.

To be black was to know pain and pride, to wear that pain with respect and to only allow the pride of that pain to shine though. Now black identity is viewed with a variable dose of disdain. Since blacks first learned about white skin, they have been fascinated with it, to the point that black people sometimes fry their hair and bleach their skin in an effort to fade from being black.

Blacks are fighting a battle with themselves - a battle to the death. Why?

White. In some instances whites are in the same position as blacks: the blender. Whites are mixing more with other races. The white woman is pursuing mixed race relationships due to love and want, be it drugs, gang wealth, or the goal to be *different*. The white woman has chosen to mix with whomever respects her body type, no matter how much she may deviate from the style icons of the day. She does not want to be the woman who does not fit the white male ideal of the beautiful and perfect female physique. She has a sense of honor to the women that came before her, the woman that wanted more from a relationship than children.

The future of whites is more secure than that of blacks, because whites have specialized groups that tend to value purity of the races. Although Jews will mix with other races, they usually prefer to marry other

Jewish people, not out of hatred, but rather to cling to their beliefs. Arabs practice the same idea: their religion requires them to stick closely together in a clan-like or tribal way, often through intermarriage with distant relatives or competitors' family members. In the white supremacy group, family mixing of races can cause death, but with great power comes great loss, and whites have the most to lose.

With the green race (money) being the race they seem most comfortable with, it will be their undoing, and the undoing of centuries of historical and cultural development.

Whites sell treasures at a steady rate: Beer companies, buildings, companies, and they even borrow against the country itself. The children of those who built America are allowing the children of their ancestors' peers to force them into selling the lifeblood of their ancestors for a few dollars more.

The love of money is the root of all evil, as the saying goes. The way whites are selling America's origins, the white soul will turn green. The souls of those that built America are fading away.

Is "money" the root of all evil? At a closer glance, maybe not so much. For whites, money is only a way to look past the people of the bottom - the people that whites used to do the work that had to be done, just not by them. So for the love of money to be the root of all evil, it has to have some type of power. For it to have power it has to be considered as an entity, because money is not alive. So where does this power or evil come from?

From whites.

Whites give money power, and everyone follows their lead. So money is not the root of all evil.

Fear is the true evil. While whites give money its power, that power comes from fear, and why does the rest of the world follow the white lead? White power generates fear. Fear has found a life of its own - a life given to it by the masses. Fear makes money grand. Fear will give courage to the meekest, and their white power will shine though. From the beginning whites will gain power though their fear, and the fear they evoke in others. It was not until money – economic currency – came into fashion that white power flourished and flooded the plains of every mind. The rush to gain favor and power over the masses starts the money race, a race that has divided white into four classes:

1. The have mores. These white were born into money and power.
2. The acquire mores. They are born into wealth and have the willingness to sell it.
3. The work mores. They acquire more; family is second to business; more is never

enough.

4. The do mores. They are not willing to share; they think all can pull themselves up, gaining more status and power/though whatever means with fewer morals.

Fear of not having enough money is a testament to where the races are and to where the races are going. How did they get to this point, the selling of white soul and the erasing of blackness? As the story goes: once upon a time in a land far, far away….

Chapter 1:   Religion vs. Faith

Jose' De Acosta, 16th century Jesuit missionary in Latin America, referred to the New World native people in this way:

> …*barbarians ignorant of faith, literary culture are unfit for self-rule; they can be considered NATURE'S SERVANTS, and civilized Christians should rule them.*

De Acosta's attitude represents what would become the common view of Europeans who came to the West Indies – and subsequently to North America and South America – to conquer and plunder the indigenous peoples for personal gain and rewards. There was no recognition of the natives' religious practices except to term them primitive and superstitious. The white explorers brought a religious system that did not encompass native peoples, but rather served as justification for enslaving and abusing them.

Over the ensuing centuries, European settlers increased in number and colonized the North American seaboard, eventually moving inland to take by force the lands and goods of native people, if they could not swindle these resources from them. Slavery was introduced by Christopher Columbus and continued to be instituted by Europeans as free labor to develop the land they claimed for their respective nations.

European enslavement of Native Americans began with Columbus. As the governor of Hispaniola, he forced the Taino Indians to labor in the Spanish fields and mines, and he brought Taino slaves to Spain on his return journeys. About 50,000 Taino died within two years of Columbus's arrival, and by 1510 the Taino population had declined by nearly 90%, primarily from European diseases but also from brutal treatment. A new source of forced labor was required. In 1518 the Spanish king allowed the importation of slaves directly from Africa (previously they had been Spanish-born Africans), and the Atlantic slave trade to the western hemisphere began in earnest, finally ending over three centuries later with the abolition of slavery in Brazil in 1888. (National Humanities Center

http://nationalhumanitiescenter.org/pds/amerbegin/settlement/settlement.htm)

This imbalance of power established the foundation of the relationship between black and white in North America. The terms *faith* and *Christian* will play a prominent role in the greed and self-destruction of black and white in the nation that would later be known as America, or the United States. Where did this thinking come from? Jose` De Acosta did not come to this conclusion by himself - it started long before he breathed life into those words. After the native Indians had been conquered and destroyed, the next group of people to be enslaved for personal enrichment were Africans brought to North America for this purpose.

The wide-scale enslavement movement needed justification for funding and propaganda support. Like the native people before them, blacks were depicted in news reports and travel letters as subhuman, irrational, and in need of control by whites. Why on life's stage is black always playing the role of villain? From the origins of the Judeo-Christian tradition inherent in the Bible scriptures, black was doomed to play a game it could never win: the white rise to power.

> *In the beginning, God created the heaven and the earth. And the earth*
>
> *was without form, and void; and darkness was upon the face of the deep. And*
>
> *the spirit of God moved upon the face of the waters. And God said, Let there*
>
> *be light: and there was light. And God saw the light, that it was good: and*
>
> *God divided the light from the darkness.* (Genesis 1:1-3 KJV)

Now, if this is your belief, then this is where light took its first step away from the darkness. And maybe this is where white started to look away from his dark-skinned brother. This could be where black would start a race to catch white, as the night starts its chase to catch the day. White will forever be referred to as the light, but the flesh will be called white - although WHITE is not their skin color. And dark skin will always be referred to as BLACK - and black will be the name of a people, even if black is not their skin color.

In the beginning as it is today, religion played a pivotal role in race relations. When the masses needed to keep the races separated, they used religion: "My god is better than yours."

When there was land that needed to be taken, it was done in the name of religion: "You do not know my god, so I will take your land for my god, and you can work it."

When slaves were needed and taken by force, it was done in the name of religion: "Ignorant of faith or ignorant of my faith, then you shall be enslaving."

Therefore, did God put black at the bottom of the ethnic and socio-economic pile? Was it God that gave black such a setback that it would take thousands of years to comfortably file behind the masses at the end of the line? Was it God's plan that black was to be the world's servant - or has the message been altered to fit the need?

These questions follow the white rise to power. The absence of answers will be the reasoning to keep black in the back: "God's will." While some whites will convince others that it is the will of God that the races be separate, not all will share this view, and this will help to spark the biblical beginning of the black-white conflict.

Not all white wanted to be separate, but many did; some insisted from the viewpoint of education that whites deserved to be taught while blacks could not comprehend learning. Others pointed to specific religious beliefs that set the races apart. A few were more open-minded, but they mainly just wanted to mate. The majority just did not want to mix any part of their lives with black blood. White did accept other races, to a point, for blood mixing. But most whites clung to their religious beliefs that teach harmony without equality.

In the beginning, the Judeo-Christian religion taught that black skin was a curse from God.

Why?

The power given to white is evident from the beginning of biblical time. God formed man from the dust, placed him in the Garden of Eden, and made for him a woman helpmate, and no matter how bad white disappointed the Creator, still there will be reasons to continue to give to him and protect him. Black was never allowed to be seen in a light that shone brighter.

While in the Garden of Eden, Adam and Eve lived in paradise, with only one restriction: do not eat from the Tree of Knowledge of Good and Evil. God's first attempt at granting humans and free will would end in the first of many disappointments. Adam and

Eve were the first humans to disappoint, and there is no biblical knowledge to say Adam and Eve were white, white claimed them. Thus, white can be seen as getting started on the biblical wrong foot. Their betrayal of God's directive would give rise to the first creature of hate, the snake. Since biblical teaching claims the serpent was Satan, snakes would be reviled like only one other created being - black.

White disappoints - snake gets the punishment. White living in paradise with everything at their command is duped into losing it all, duped by a serpent, and so the beginning of white greed is born - the first branch of greed to grow on the white family tree. This was the first of many punishments followed by forgiveness given by God to white. Eve allowed a serpent to corrupt her; Adam allowed his helpmate to corrupt him. The first woman was given her punishment for this violation:

"I will greatly multiply thy sorrow and thy conception."

And to Adam:

"Cursed is the ground for thy sake; in sorrow shalt thou eat of it all the days of thy life."

In defending themselves, Adam blames the woman and the woman blames the snake. The serpent did not give or was not given the opportunity to blame anyone or anything; it simply took its punishment.

Black is not yet described as being on earth. In time black will enter the biblical land, and a black woman will suffer for the misdeed of a white woman. A black man will not get to step foot in paradise. So from this biblical standpoint, at this time black lost out on the opportunity to see how good and easy life could have been. A black man is punished for things not of his making. Not getting to see paradise is a mustard seed compared to the punishment the black woman would endure - painful child birth; a product of white disobedience.

After eating from the forbidden Tree, Adam and Eve learn of their nakedness and subsequently explored sex. This would institute the natural family roles and structure, along with the mandate for man to work hard all his days and woman to bear children in great pain. Cast out of the Garden of Eden, the pair had to be responsible for themselves. Beyond the now-forbidden Garden of Eden, the first couple had children, Cain and Abel. Between these two brothers came jealousy, anger, and murder:

> "And God said unto Cain, 'Where is Abel thy brother?"
>
> "And he said, 'I know not: am I my brother's keeper?"
>
> "And God said, 'What hast thou done? The voice of my brother's blood
>
> cried unto me from the ground…and now art thou cursed from the earth,
>
> which hath opened her mouth to receive thy brother's blood from thy hand."

Such was the first murder committed by the first family's first child.

While some think Eve committed the first disobedience of God's command, it could be said that the angels disobeyed before that. During an earlier war in Heaven, Satan was expelled from Heaven, taking a third of the heavenly host (angels) with him. He then presented a temptation to Eve, as the serpent. While the debate can go on indefinitely, the truth is that because of Eve, God will continue throughout the Bible to be disappointed in the progress of his creation. While women will bear the curse of childbirth, men will be given a biblical slap on the wrist - a fact that will follow white into the twenty-first century. Cain, out of greed for God's affection and approval, killed Abel his brother and was cursed. What was the curse? Facile scar or skin color.

Why does it matter? This event helps us to get a picture of where black stood in the early years of religious history, to see if black had a firm footing, or if God placed white above him, as he had done with Adam being over the other created beings - animals. Abel's death had consequences for Cain, which was God's curse, but the Bible does not say what the curse would be. Some have stated that black skin was the curse given from god. The Bible states that there was a curse and a mark. Some blend the two. Why? Was it to find a way to blame black for white biblical shortcomings? Was it to elevate white above black? Early Christians, Jews, and Muslims all believe some truth of the curse being black skin. Later the Mormons would start a new version of Christianity and teach it to be fact, just not to be spoken of as fact. What if God did give Cain black skin? Then Cain should be the black father to all men. Cain was sent into the wilderness with God's promise that whosoever slayed Cain, vengeance would be taken on that person sevenfold.

With black skin, Cain started a city. With black skin, Cain gave birth to a nation. When his offspring's skin started to lighten for whatever reason, once again light will be separate from the darkness, as God had done in the beginning. If black skin was God's way of punishing Cain, then God thought white was better. Why? When religion is viewed at a glance, there is God and there is white. Cain killed Abel: God first cursed Cain, then protected him, and then educated him well enough to build a city and start a family nation, which was another slap on the wrist for man. Were these first people white? Was the curse truly black skin? No one knows for sure. The only thing one knows for sure (or at least as sure as one can be) is that the Middle East is the likely start for the three main world religions, and with the regional inhabitants' appearance today, maybe it is what they look like then, which is more white than black.

Fast-forward past Adam, Eve, Cain, and Abel. God still gives favorable treatment to white. Noah will build a great ark to prepare for a world-wide flood; he and his family will be the sole survivors. Afterward, the drink (wine) called to him and re-introduced sin into the world, symbolizing a watery grave that meets the unbeliever. From the beginning of biblical time God has continued to serve white, all while only a small fraction of whites truly served him. Time and again, whites repaid favor with one disappointment after another.

The Egyptians gave the world most of its written and architectural civility, along with the Roman and Greeks. The Egyptians gave the world paper, commerce, and farming, all through the grace of God. But what god did they give their thanks to? Many: Re, Rennutet, Isis, Horus, Osiris. Ancient Egypt worshipped too many gods, god of nature and humans; they worshipped for harvest, health, and war. So why didn't the Egyptians know about the god that was on his way to free the people the Egyptians were enslaving? The "why" cannot be known for sure. What is known is that some early Egyptians had dark skin and dark hair. What is known biblically is that God was coming to deal with the Egyptians in favor of their slaves, the Israelites. Was the Israelite nation truly slaves in the sense that they were owned? It is said that the Egyptians grew fearful of the number of Israelites so they dealt with them harshly. As slaves, couldn't their number be controlled? The dark-skinned Egyptian would bring about the wrath of God for their decision, the decision to harshly deal with the Israelite. Why was the number a reason for fear? The fear could have been the need to be in control and not to share their wealth. Egypt had created a need to be taken care of: wealth, which is early evidence of money being the root of all evil.

Maybe Egypt also is where slavery started, if the Israelites were truly enslaved, or just worked as slaves with the treatment of a slave. Slave or not, God would be their

Emancipator and Moses would give the proclamation: "Let my people go!" And after God's version of arm-twisting, the Egyptians did let their slaves go, but did they go as freed slaves or as people with the greatest of protectors - or did they leave as a people preparing for the wars to come? On their way out the Israelites borrowed or took enough to live in the desert for forty years, to supplement the manna that God would later send.

Why is this important to race relations in the U.S.? It shows how war and the enslavement of people make whites stand above all and it shows how far black has come. From the biblical beginning, blacks started out with nothing, and while something is small to white, it should be considered something to black. While it is said that all peoples have been slaves at one time or another, for the most part other slave have had features that remind their owner of themselves; it could be readily seen by their capture, all save for one, black. Never in the history of the world has one race not had a relationship built on religion, only black. Never in the history has one race been so separate from all other. Why?

Then there is only one race that would be directly secured by the Almighty. After years of calling on God to relieve their suffering, God sent Moses to save the Israelite slaves. Moses was already in their midst. That Moses would be the speaker for God. While God would not talk to his chosen few or their capturer, God would speak to Moses. Moses will do what has to be done. God would not make it easy on the children of Israel, but he will teach the most painful lesson to Pharaoh. As Pharaoh found the power of the God of Abraham hard to accept, he tried to use logic to account for the power of the Israelite's God. God's power was also hard for the Israelite to comprehend; their prayers was being answered by a power they could not fathom. After several demonstrations of his God-given power, Moses won the fear of Pharaoh. Pharaoh's education could not stop the power of the God of Moses. While giving in to Moses meant allowing the slaves to go, it was the power of their God that bent the Egyptian to see the testament of Moses's God. The death and plague that God sent into the land of the Egyptian for the security of the Israelites will be quickly forgotten. Complaining will follow the Israelites for years. No matter the favor and salvation sent by God, complaining will be the Israelites' only comfort.

Still, Moses pressed on with the instructions given to him by God. From walking through the Red Sea to having their hunger quenched in the desert, still the chosen people's faith waned. Everything that did not go perfectly meant that complaining followed, rather than gratitude.

While on their way to the Promised Land, God gave them the Ten Commandments of how they should live. There were additional guidelines for how to process their food, and a host of other lifestyle sanctity issues. With all Moses was charged with doing, he would disappoint God as had the Israelites. Moses would lead his people to the land of milk and honey, but not get there himself. With all that was done for the Israelite, it would not be all, as God would continue to assist them in battles great and small. All was done for the children of Abraham, and in most cases, they were not pleasing to their God. And God would deal harshly with his disobedient children.

While the power of Abraham's God was great, he did not just free the people of Israel; he put his power on display for the Egyptians. In a word, he tortured the Egyptians:

> "And the Lord said unto Moses, 'When thou goest to return into Egypt, see that thou do all those wonders before Pharaoh, which I have put in thine hand: but I will harden his heart, that he shall not let the people go.'"

Why? What is known is that some Egyptians had dark skin and dark hair. They were perhaps the originators of the African race. God punished them severely for enslaving the Israelites. Does that long-ago punishment hang over black-skinned people today?

The Egyptian allows riches and Israelite numbers to cloud their judgment as to the treatment of the slaves under their care. The Israelite could not keep their faith while under the yoke of a slave master. Moses would allow (some think) the constant complaining of the Israelites to allow his faith in God to wane; this weakness will allow him only to see the Promised Land, but not enter. As far as the beginning of the Bible in the Old Testament goes, black is seldom mentioned. However, there is the story of Ham, Noah's son, the one that would be cursed, along with his descendants - and not by God but by his father. Once again, blacks take a step to the back of the faith-based line.

> "And the Lord said unto me: "Prophesy"; and I prophesied, saying:
>
> 'Behold the people of Canaan, which are numerous, shall go forth in
> battle array against the people of Shum, and shall slay them that they shall
> utterly be destroyed; and the people of Canaan shall divide themselves in
> the land, and the land shall be barren and unfruitful, and none other people
> shall dwell there but the people of Canaan...'
>
> For behold, the Lord shall curse the land with much heat, and the
> barrenness thereof shall go forth forever; and there was a blackness came
> upon all the children of Canaan, that they were despised among all
> people."

As God's chosen few fail repeatedly, there is still no or very little mention of black. There is a mentioning of Moses being married to a woman from Ethiopia, a woman his brother did not seem to approve of, and she could have been black. With all the violence in the Old Testament, still very little is known about black in the time of Moses. Even the slaves in the Bible are not black. The closest thing to black is Egyptian, and they had no favor with God. Could it be that they did not treat God's chosen few favorably? Could it be that they chose to pit their god against the God of Abraham, their idols against the idol of the children of Abraham? After numerous accounts of God's power, still the Egyptian needed more proof. After getting the proof, was it then true that the Egyptian gods were false, and of no real value? Why would God tease the Egyptians with knowledge only to have it betray them when it was truly needed? However wrong the Egyptian might have been, the Israelites were not so easily persuaded that they were godly enough. God's proof was not readily accepted by all his chosen people. With everything that was shown to both Israelis and Egyptians, still men would live ungodly. The truth is all civilization believes in some form of higher power. The Egyptian worshipped the sun and also animal gods. It wasn't until Moses went to God and showed the Israelites the god that they had prayed to, the God of Abraham, that they believed. Still others believed in nature gods or reincarnation. Some would not be shown the god of the Israelites for years to come.

"God so loved the world that he gave his only begotten son": enter the New Testament. Is this true? And what does it mean? Some think that God so love humans that he sent his son to give humans a key into heaven. However, could it also mean that God so loved the earth, his first creation - the one that was never destroyed – that it is the one that his second creation is and has always been in conflict with? God so loved the world that he gave humankind reason and the means to be stewards of the world. Possible? Could it be that God so loved the earth that he gave himself or herself the legitimate clause to destroy humans?

With Noah, God allowed him to be ridiculed and mocked, all while preparing to send rain down on the scoffers. Not even the black raven Noah sent to find dry land would succeed. It would be the white dove with the olive branch that people remember. Noah's youngest son would see the nakedness of his father and be punished – cursed to be the servant to all. Not the first son, but the youngest. Would this be the second father of blacks?

The Bible teaches how animals are to be killed, how crimes are to be dealt with. It shows the miracles done by God; it shows all but precious little about how black should be treated, with lots of room for interpretation. It showed how God never abandons the Israelite. It showed how no matter how much God gave white, they wanted more, or never truly appreciated their blessing. Throughout history whites have had an unfair advantage over other races. Some even had advantages over other whites. But all in all black never had anything other than what was given to them by white. White has never quite lived up to the religion they claimed to practice; while being Christian they have taken what they wanted, taken what they needed. Always reaping great wealth, all while creating great grief. Whites have fought in the name of religion and forced their practices on others, not thinking of the consequences, just wanting to be right. These religious wars will rival any death of any war for old fashion conquest. Most pray to the same god to get help in fighting each other, and when the victory is at hand, they feel vindicated. God chose their side so God must approve of their actions. They have been heard to say that they are doing God's work, never pausing to think that God should not need help, and the fact that their God needs help is only showing how weak their god is; their Almighty cannot be almighty at the help of flesh and blood of man. With all the land, power, and respect one would think they would be looking to share God's gifts. No. White takes what it wants, and what been taken from them they will move heaven and earth to get back. They are in no way looking to start a Garden of Eden of their own. White is simply looking to acquire as much as their lives will allow. From in the beginning to now, white have found many ways to not live up to the promise God made with their ancestors; God made the promise; they did not make a promise to God to live up to the promise he made to them. The Ten Commandments are broken still today; whites still enslave citizen, using the Bible as a first century ATM machine, and it is as common now as in the first century.

In Sodom and Gomorrah God saw fit to destroy the key towns of the plain of Moab.

With the Egyptians, God not only got the Israelites out of bondage but also tortured the Egyptians.

The New Testament contains less violence, except when it comes to Jesus's death. Yet, the New Testament is not widely accepted by God's chosen few. Most Israelites do not follow the teaching of the New Testament. They are not reasonably able to follow the meaning of Jesus's life and teachings. The reason for the creation of Jesus is so all people can be accepted into the Kingdom of the Lord. The fact that God had done all he did for the Israelites with little to show for his effort meant that God decided he would now show all humans his power and give all who desired the path to everlasting life. With God's constant need to destroy, rebirth, and rebuild humanity, he offered a key, knowing that we would need either no free will or a means to repent our sins, and God chose the path of least resistance. Give humans a role model like themselves: Jesus will live and die for our sake. Not all will believe in him and not all will accept the fact that his only reason for being here was to die and then rise again. Some will blame the Jews for the death of Jesus (which they should champion and not blame) for doing the thing that God sent Jesus here for. The New

Testament is a little different toward blacks than the Old Testament. Still there is the statement that slaves should obey their masters.

Very little about organized religion relates to black, but black are proud to be called Christian, the religion that showed the black race as beneath the white. This is the religion that allows Bible readers to twist and pull its words to handicap other races. It allows leaders to commit whatever transgressions they need to, all under the umbrella of what God thinks or says, or what God wants. When black is taught any history, they do not have leading roles. When black is taught any religion, they are not the leaders. How can any race of people feel worthy of having anything good happen in their lives, when they are second in everything? When even God did not see fit to give them anything special, only limited skills? All through the Bible, God protects, God kills, God speaks, and God condemns. Most often, the condemning is either to blacks, or to someone else to whom he has simply given too much and not gotten any appreciation.

One would think, why didn't black start its own religion? Black has its own religion, but for the most part blacks are afraid to practice it.

Voodoo! Out of Africa comes this spirit-driven religion - the religion that requires the participant to enter a trance. The religion that frightens the worshipper as much as the non-worshipper, at least after whites modified it with dolls and movies.

Voodoo: Blacks getting no visit from God would start what is now commonly thought of as superstition or devil worship. Only the true practitioner knows or cares to know the difference. When things went wrong, black had little knowledge, so if a woman came new to the tribe and the crop failed, she could be killed. If the tribe elder could not find a simple answer to a complex question, then something had to be burned; someone had to die.

And everything could be a cause for death. In some cases, the elder did know but chose to keep it to himself to keep his position of power and ability to exploit the other tribesmen. Power is the only thing that makes all men equal. The power to exploit each other must be the devil's doing? The thing that tribesman did come to understand was done without the hand-holding that God gave to white. The cures, the accidental cures that black stumbled onto, could be the effect of God intervening, but if so, why so little? If not, why not?

Voodoo was black finding faith, looking to forefather and foremother to guide them. This would lead to conflict and not be tolerated when blacks reached the New World. The course of black life and black place in America would directly follow the gift-giving of God to white, black will be yet another form of Eden for whites to do with what they will. When the New Testament came to black eyes, it came from white. Black did not read so white read to them, explaining how even God wanted them to be less than white. Still, black put their faith in this book, all while seeing whites violate it on a daily basis. Black gave and continue to give Jesus the honor and the glory. Still, while whites were bearing witness to the power of God, black were simply there to feel the effect. While Jesus has almost replaced the God of Abraham in the eyes of most Christians and some Jews alike, there are still rumbles that Jesus was only a way to tone down barbaric behavior still practiced by people some white didn't want to be associated with. Even Jesus did not talk to blacks, did not walk on water near blacks, and did not change water to wine for blacks. So why is black so beholden to a religion that has only given them a subsistence after paving the streets with gold for white? The same reason black does most thing; they do what it takes to acknowledge the power of the white life.

Sunday morning is the most segregated day of the week. Why? Why is it that worshippers of the same god need to do so out of the view of others? Blacks like the music. White just needs the word. All religion has basically the same belief: A god and a prophet, and most believe that God loves all, and God protects all. Then there are those that believe there is the one true religion, and everyone else is going to hell or some other undesirable place; some even think that it is their own personal responsibility to send all who do not share their belief to the undesirable place. Still others think that even if you believe in what they believe, if it is not practiced as they practice, then time is wasted and the undesirable place awaits them. You cannot have love problem or clothes issues, or you are wasting God's time and theirs.

How can so many religions even exist? Simple: everyone want to teach things their way. Black wants to blend in, so adopting the one thing that is most responsible for the black condition was never in doubt. Was religion responsible for the black condition? Directly, no, but with white interpretation, it was indirectly, and not just Christianity, but all the major religions, all have written something that has either degraded or hinted at the inferiority of black skin. When Columbus "discovered" the New World, religion comes too. The great Greek philosopher Aristotle, long dead, will haunt blacks with his understanding of the plight of the uneducated. Aristotle's theory was that some people were naturally slaves and some were naturally masters, so men rule naturally over women and Greeks rule naturally over Barbarians. *Barbarian* is a Greek term first used to describe someone not Greek. Later it was used to discriminate. Juan Gines De Sepulveda, Jose' De Acosta, and Bishop De Las Casas will set the time and date for the arrival and treatment of the black race. De Sepulveda and De Acosta will argue that the ignorant should serve the enlightened. They will use the Bible and the ancient words of Aristotle to argue the enslavement of the natives of South American and islander, the ones they incorrectly called Indian. This will lead to the doorstep of black. Bishop De Las Casas developed compassion for the natives and fought to get them some relief. The compassion for the native would be pain for black, who were being used as slaves in other areas, including but not limited to Spain. The only difference is the unforeseen rise of the United State of America. With no godly intervention, the descendent of Adam or Cain or Ham would become the servant of the world. But…

What if the primordial ooze is your idea of Eden? What if Charles Darwin is your idea of a prophet? What if you believe that millions of years ago debris from a cosmic explosion dropped into the water of the new-forming earth and caused a cosmic soup from which all manner of creatures developed? Could you still get into heaven if you were wrong? Some think not! Therefore, what if you were the one that was right? Was religion a waste of time? When the effect of religion is study, the righteous are found to have more of a generally healthy life, grief is shorter, and problem-handling is easier. The all-around faithful are generally content. What about the evolutionist? On the one hand they have only the fact and test to comfort them, while some straddle the fence to cover their bases; others are 99.99 percent sure that they are the ones that will prove to be right. At least, mostly right. Still, Charles Darwin did find some very interesting things. One he did not find, however, is why black would be dealt a losing hand.

When black is looking at life from a religious viewpoint, it seems as if God him/herself is against them. In all the major religions, nowhere is black given so much as a thought. So why not look to science or the nature of science as it relates to evolution: the notion that all men are created equal. White wrote the Bible, Torah, and Koran, or at least translated it. The people that God talked to were some other skin color than dark brown. So maybe they took a few liberties with the fact to make them look as if God was on their side. However, nature is not on the side of any person. Right?

Chapter 2: FROM ADAM TO SLAVE or APE TO SLAVE

Although most experts believe that the rise of religion began in the Middle East where people looked more white than black, faith of a spiritual nature started when early man began to reason.

Let's examine the findings of Charles Darwin (1809-1882), English biologist, geologist, and naturalist. Who is smarter: white or black?

White.

Why?

Nature.

When Darwin took his ship voyage, he was given pause to use the greatest gift nature ever bestowed on white; curiosity. Darwin was curious why birds from similar islands had such different adaptations. His curiosity moved to plants and other animals, all similar in design, but all with subtle differences. When he published *Origin of Species by Means of Natural Selection or the Preservation of the Favored Races in the Struggle for Life* (1859), he outlined the failure of black in print. Natural Selection chose white to be the brain of the operation, and black - the muscle. The why is not known, but climate had to have played a role.

The fact is indisputable. The evidence of white rise to power is in any museum that can be visited. The path is written in every history book, and chronicled in countless films.

An estimated guess of 4.2 million years ago reveals that in Ethiopia an animal with human-like movement - or at least movement different from other apes that roamed the tropical savannas of what one day would be labeled Africa - Ardipithecus Ramids lived. An estimated guess of 3.2 million years ago, Australopithecus Afarensis, or Lucy, lived. These are the oldest fossils found to date and thought to be the oldest, or earliest, human-like remains (although some do not believe this is where humans originated) found in an area south of the biblical origins: Found by white, giving white the means to declare to the world his view; found by white because black for the most still lacks a great deal of curiosity. If Ardi was the first attempt of nature to bring humans into the fold of earthly inhabitants, then one could say that humans or what would one day be human was first walking around Ethiopia, one of only a few African places in the Bible (black Africa).

The skin beneath the animal hair could have been white or black; fossils cannot tell for sure. What is certain is Ardi and Lucy died out, along with their descendants. Ardi and Lucy did leave nature with a blue-print to start again, and nature did indeed start over, with Homo hablis, the new generation that was less ape and more human. Homo hablis was the tool-making human, more human yet ape thinking. Homo-hablis was still a hunter / gatherer, as were Lucy and Ardi (probably), but Nature saw fit to increase the brain size, and in doing so making Homo hablis the ruler over other animals, or at least better able to kill and process them. Still Homo hablis wasn't quite ready to adopt all human qualities, so back to the lab went Mother Nature, and then enter Homo erectus. Nature came up with a version of species much more distinctive than the common ape; this version walked upright, with better mobility, greater vision, and the ability to view the hunting field farther and better. This branch of human development had less hair and dark skin.

What happened? Nature made a choice.

Why did black rise not mirror white's rise? The answer is in the fossil record.

When white was black, they rose supreme over all species. As one troop of ape-like creature grew, they all grew; when nature handed out the ability to make tools, all could make tools. When nature endowed the ability to walk upright, all walked upright.

Then something happened. One troop of early humans was given something different, something that was not given to all that dwelt in sub-Sahara Africa. The reasoning is not known, but the outcome would separate black and white forever, or almost forever.

Curiosity.

When nature bestowed curiosity on one group of early humans and not the other, it assured that one would lead and one would follow. The skin color would also be the color of the loser. The color of dread - as early humans must have dreaded the night. Black would dread the outcome of a simple hunger, not of the stomach, but of the mind. As clever as early man was, nature chose one over the other. While Ardipithecus Ramids was or could be the mother tree of all humans, better branches started to appear in the fossil record. Some Homo erectus not only had the ability to walk upright, but also had been imbued with curiosity. With it he walked out of Africa and into the role of leader.

Enter Cro-Magnon. While Lucy may have dragged her knuckles on the ground, the next step in nature's plan was to create a human that walked upright and had a bigger brain. At this point there is no white gap in thinking; the tool used by early humans could be found all over. The mobility factor of the upright walker and curiosity will soon come into play, soon meaning centuries. The bigger brain, coupled with increased mobility, only gave nature the idea to start with humans that could walk upright. Homo sapiens would hand down a legacy that would create a bigger brain: the greater thinker, the better builder, the new and improved Homo erectus. With what is known and not known, the early human record is a guessing game, brought to life by clues such as ancient housing, tools, pots, other cookery, and hunting equipment, which is what Homo hablis left behind. Homo hablis fossils have been found outside of sub-Saharan Africa, meaning that whites were roaming other parts of the earth. The troop of Homo hablis that was moving out of sub-Sahara Africa would be the troop to shed its black skin. The wonderment given to this troop began to move them forward into locales they occupy today.

Moving out of southern Africa with a bigger brain and more brain power led to the birth of reasoning power: The ability to create and to move, to wonder. While one troop of hablis was wondering what else the earth had to offer, the other was keeping close to what was familiar and must be done now. One troop wanted to discover what was over the next horizon or around the next tree, as well as what danger they could get in and out of. The other troop focused on danger they could get into and how to avoid it. Some went to explore the danger; still others avoided danger. So the troop that left to seek danger left behind tools, cookery, stone carving, and black skin.

The perils that early humans had to overcome started with his fear. The group that could best control fear might well be the fittest. The fittest of the two groups would be retooled. While the black hablis is not a bad model or at least not a model that needed to be destroyed, nature just allowed black hablis to grow at their own pace. That pace was glacial in comparison to the quick spurt of growth whites would have. The survival rate of one group going into the unknown must have been slim at best; the fear factor must have been off the chart. The threat of what animals to unprotected groups required great courage. The courage to stay must have been great as well, to watch others leave and not know what their station in life would be, not knowing if they were going to a better place or if the place was going to be even more dangerous. Did the group that stayed really have courage? Was it bravery that made them stay? And what of the ones that left - was that courage? Could food or weather be the force driving the decision? What reason was there to leave? And why wasn't it compelling enough for all to leave? Or all to stay? And why go so far that coming back was not an option? These questions will never be answered; the answer died with Homo hablis. Homo sapiens would try only to live better through the knowledge Homo hablis left behind.

Homo sapiens: wise men. Homo hablis left east Africa, conquered his fear, and used all the brain power at his command, but still he slipped into oblivion. Nature would praise his effort by allowing him to morph into a new human, Homo sapiens. With all the knowledge of the preceding prototype, the Homo sapiens would give rise to the upgraded human. The next step in evolution would come with the means to use forethought. With this upgrade, human learned to use the brain in ways never before seen, at least not in the fossil record. Now instinct will give way to planning. An upgrade in thinking would increase movement as well as improve tools and weapons. This gave rise to modern white. Developing the ability to withstand all that nature put them through, modern white would be rebuilt over and over to evolve to the white of today.

Neanderthal. The appearance of Neanderthals in colder climate meant that clothes were not just casual covering but absolutely necessary. Even hunting had a different value: eat or die. Make warm clothes or die. The Neanderthal with a full stomach would freeze just as surely as a hungry one would. Clothing in early humans was optional and minimal; it wasn't a matter of life or death. Today it is still optional in certain parts of Africa. This would not be so to the evolving incarnation of man. The farther north whites moved, the more of a necessity clothes became. Clothing would come to identify savages from so-called non-savages. Neanderthal in his new climate would wage constant war with weather and hunger. With food and clothing so important to white and the ability to adapt to his environment, nature rewarded him with a gift, a passion for war.

Early humankind was more interested in learning their place in the world, learning how to avoid being eaten, and procreating. Very little is known about early war, but Neanderthal fossils have been found to have died of other than natural causes. Groups needed to hunt together, but the group could not get so big as to out-hunt the prey. So war was needed. In the eastern part of Africa, the weather would have been mild, with generally fair conditions year round, so food was more plentiful there, meaning there was little need for war. This would not be as pleasing as is it sounds, for what early black gained in peace, later black would pay for in blood and sweat. In a battle with a hostile climate, hostile competition, hostile animals, this will give white a lust for war. It's wisdom in battle. It's fearlessness of hostile climate and its claim to the world, a claim that will emerge after another incarnation.

Cro-Magnon. This human ancestor would take or receive (no one knows which) the mantle of overseer over the planet. Cro-Magnon and Neanderthal seem to have lived around the same time. They could have been rivals, or one could have outlived or outfought the other for the right to guide modern man into his future. The two took all of nature's trail version of humans and incorporate them into the quintessential being: A white person. This version had been tried by all that came before him; only white could master what other human versions only came close to understanding. Modern whites complete what nature starts. Then with enough forethought, white left his descendant the will to benefit from all he would accomplish.

As the world changed over eons of time, the one thing that would stay the same would be the quest for more. This would bring about the need for farming, and farming would bring about the need to become more sedentary. The nomadic lifestyle would be left to the few, the ones that require little to be content.

Black. With the ability to grow crops, the hunter / gatherer becomes more of an entrepreneur. The gathering would be done from one place or from one group source. Hunting transformed into taming of animals and breeding herds. The domestication of livestock leads to the ability to trade; the domestication of wolves leads to a working dog. The wolf goes from adversary to companion, and the hunt becomes safer.

This is the trait that white would wield better than any weapon, turning an adversary into a companion and the domestication of everyone else. With farming becoming the mainstay lifestyle, land was needed. The better the land, the better the crop. The closer the water is to the land, the more this land is prime. So early man needed to control where others could live - enter land ownership. No longer is land just the earth; now it is something that could be owned and fought over. These men, the ones that owned land, will be the men that white becomes: The owner of land, the owner of property, and the owner of people. This development will bring the two halves of the first people together again, with dire consequences for one and great wealth for the other, along with great pain and shame for all. With this increased knowledge white will use the skills that nature provided him, the knowledge passed down from all the copies of the past, the ability to cultivate the soil, the wisdom to know what was good to eat and what was good to grow, and the best soils for growing certain crops. He would understand the best time to plant and the appropriate time for harvest. All this was the gift of many past creations. Neanderthal's brute strength, Homo erectus's hunting skill, Homo hablis's tool making – these were all the key ingredients that were now bearing fruit. The uncivilized mannerisms were kept hidden, but just below the surface, where it could be called upon at any time.

That early time required both black and white to shed blood for food and for survival. Now that food was grown it should have given white a calming effect, and in the short term it did. Then things changed. Instead of being calm at the thought of having, ownership became a game. What will the non-having people do for me! Now that land ownership was the way, fights broke out to possess the best. In the past, fighting over food was for the good of the family; now it was to see who could hoard the most and sell the best or get the best trade. The ability of early man to fight was needed to compete for food. The fact was that modern man had to fight, or work, to provide for wife and children. His ability to fight became great; the animal instinct needed to survive and kill melted away with the increase in brain size. No longer was there need to solve disagreements with fighting. Early modern man used reason to compromise, but the fighting skills were still there. The primitive mind would use these skills only when property was threatened. To have all that was needed (the ability to grow food, shelter, community) should have given early man the elusive utopia. But it didn't; all it gave was more to fight over.

Modern man's ability to get and keep a mate meant maintaining the ability to provide for her. With the formation of communities, women were free to mate with men they found attractive. Women were also used to attract men, to gain the favor of men to help the family. While living off the land, early women knew that the strongest would produce strong offspring, but in community living being the strongest wasn't a necessity. At least not yet. Women had more attributes to choose from in selecting a mate, and wealth was at the top of the list. This is a gift from nature to the white woman: the use of sex. The more a man had to offer, the more in demand he became. The more in demand he became, the more women wanted what he had, be it wealth or power. As modern man gained wealth, he gained the favor of women, so if he could not keep what he had, he had to pay someone to help him keep it, be it family or men looking for work. If women became mates out of love, then the man didn't have to work, but white women learned early on that love doesn't feed a family. The man must learn to trade his goods for what was needed, or trade himself.

This was the beginning of two critical components in human development: armies and slaves. The ability to get what one needed came in other ways, such as making things that others wanted or products that others needed. Being the strongest was falling out of fashion, but not for long. The ability to mix chemicals to make bronze would push humans forward. In the past, man was at the whim of nature, but now he could create things from the earth itself. No longer would man be confined to remodeling nature's gift; he now possessed the ability to produce weapons and tools out of earth's minerals. White was mixing one compound to get another. White was growing beyond nature's control.

Back down South, black was still half-dressed. While white was leaping from one incarnation to the next, black was barely moving. For every leap white made, black took a half-step. White had several different versions, each more advanced than the previous. Could nature have seen that its lighter version was the best of the experiment? Why would black not find curiosity and not get curious - not wonder where the other group went? Not want to make things? White was mixing compounds, but black was still hunting and gathering. How could both see the same sky and come to different questions? White looked to find meaning and why things were as they were. Black looked only to appreciate. With no struggle, black would not get the brain of white, at least not as quickly. Black had all that was needed to live a life of contentment. They didn't have the needs or wants of white. Black in their environment was complete. Their contentment would only become a problem when their white brothers came back to visit. Not remembering their black brothers, white set themselves on a path of progress. This progress would be fraught with bloodshed. Conquest would be the order of days to come.

In community living, power came from wealth. But wealth brought problems, and the question became - how to keep it? The past held the answer: Family. The more relatives one had, the more marriages that could be arranged, and the more that men could keep family wealth. With the increase in family, wealth had to increase. Power had to be gained. But how? Be the strongest family, be the wealthiest family, and share. Get the trust of other people; have them pay for your counsel. Have them come to you for conflict resolution. Allow them to use you, allow them to need you, then charge them. But make it their idea, and then allow them to make you the leader. Power and respect will follow. Pharaoh, Emperor, King and President.

When whites walked out of eastern Africa, they didn't walk in a straight line, nor did they all leave from the same part or end up in the same place. White spread out in all directions; they would all come back together in war. The white that was to achieve greatness first was the Egyptian. From Egypt, civilization would flourish. The Egyptian started the race to own the most, and the best. Egypt's advancement filled today's black with pride, the pride of knowing that dark-skinned people were the first people, and that the Egyptian started the race that jump- started civilization. The pride of being the first people and the ancestor of ancient Egyptians gives today's black talking points, but nothing else. Were blacks the first people? Not all will agree; the same thing can be said for the Egyptian question.

Yes, blacks are descendent of Egyptians, but no more so than white. The question that should be asked is this: Will the Egyptian claim black as a descendent? To have Egyptians as an ancestor would be a matter of honor, because Egyptians created part of civilization that we embrace today. They built cities, made paper, created architecture, established agriculture, hand-printed books, and founded basic math. No other country did earlier than Egypt. They developed a calendar - the best scholars, writers, and Egyptians would take the concept of village life to new height. The pyramids alone could be considered the height of the Egyptians empire. If they did nothing else, just the fact that they built the pyramids would make anyone proud. But this is not all they did. They could not or did not want to do the work themselves, so they obtained slaves. They could not or would not allow one ruler to easily succeed another. Like others, they allowed power and jealousy to bring them down, and they fell. But there were others to pick over their body, to claim their work to enslave or employ scholars, writers, and builders.

Enter Rome… and the undisputed white race. While Egyptians came in various hues of brown, Romans were white or Caucasian. They were the only race that came close in an attempt to build a utopia. The only drawbacks were not one race, not the Egyptians nor Greeks, or any of the other countries try to adequately compensate the workforce. From the beginning of time there has been one group trying to separate from the other, and the Romans will not be any different. The Roman will create a more thinking government, a government that would listen to hear people and attempt to conquer their fear while fulfilling their wants.

The Roman system of government has been copied to this day. Romans also took the best of the world and concentrated it in Rome; this provided them with massive armies and great knowledge. With this knowledge Rome gave birth to arrogance and debauchery, both of which swept away the greatness that Rome should have held for all time.

At this point in history, all whites have been convinced that they should rule the world, or at the very least, have more than the person that came before them. All are convinced that the power and respect they seek to find will be the final leg of a never-ending journey. Because of their arrogance, each Emperor thought they could possess the love of the common people, each believing they could do a better job than the ruler before them. All thought that the emperor's wealth and power would be easy to get and manageable to control. Rome's great wealth and powerful army shone a great light on its arrogance. While Rome's army knew war, as did all white, Rome simply knew it better than most. What they knew and what they didn't know was equal in importance: How to share? What to do with soldier between wars? How to keep the fury to kill without it escaping to kill the leader of the one that needed killing done on their behalf. They knew that anything worth having could be bought or taken at the point of a sword. What they didn't understand was all whites possessed the passion to have and not all be swayed by Roman trinkets, from the meek to strong, white will battle Rome.

Barbarians at the gates. The barbarians wreaked havoc on the northern part of Africa and all over northern Europe. With the light gleaming off the spoils of war held by the Romans, all wanted their share. Goths, hired for various battles by the Romans, were misused in peace by the Romans and forced to beg for what should have been payment. The primitive mind of white is never far away; the white that knows death. Rome will make the mistake most powerful people make - underestimating the common people. Rome's problem with this thinking is forgetting about the jealousy factor. The conceit of several Roman rulers needed the mantra of Spiderman: "With great power comes great responsibility." This could have served Rome as well as her entire army. The sight of great wealth is gravity defined; the pull of wealth is as great as the pull of the moon on the oceans. Partner that with a feeling of inadequacy, and resentment starts to show. The soldier knowing he has a family to care for and the Roman with a family to care for - the Roman gets the lion share of the profit, and the soldier gets the lion share of the work, which makes for an uneasy partnership at best. Knowing that the way the wealthy won their riches at the point of a sword implied that the only way to get was to give pain, and not just pain as you've seen others give it, but primal pain. And that is what the Goths brought to the Romans. Rome kept its foot on the back of the Goths, only allowing them to acquire so much; they needed the Goths to be indebted to them. The Romans knew that if they were pushed they would push back, so why did they not think that the same could be said of any white?

Emperor after Emperor failed at achieving a lasting peace; some failed in providing adequate representation after their death; still others would fail to adequately compensate the people. Some would simply not be up to the task put on their often-young shoulders. Peaceful travelers would often visit Rome, but like tourists of today, never for long - long as in the term of "Rome existent". As the Goths rampaged through Rome, it would not be the first or the last time that someone would get Rome's attention.

Vandals. The Vandals would not be the best, but they would make a name for themselves. They would plunge Rome into a spiral that would spin the second great civilization into the abyss. To *vandalize* is to pay homage to the Vandals; their brutal tactics still appear in the twenty-first century as an adjective to describe the worst misbehavior. Like the Goths, Vandals would go on a bloodthirsty rampage, conquering all that opposed them. They spread throughout Europe, but they were barbarians, mostly illiterate, and nomadic. The Romans were ill equipped to handle such barbaric behavior. While the Romans could get as brutal as any enemy, they preferred to fight as an army, soldier to soldier and army to army. They wanted to civilize killing, making it unlike murder. This is why what was done to them was known as a barbaric attack. What they did to others was known as an invasion.

The climate, coupled with weather, one of the catalysts that propelled whites to the hierarchy, forced another group of barbarians to plunder.

Vikings. The Vikings were not living in an ideal climate, causing one group of Vikings to constantly attack the other. The transferring of meager rations from one poor to the other forced the Viking to make what would be the second most important voyage in human history, the first being the trip from Africa.

Long ships. While Rome was a powerful enemy, it was constantly tested. The long ship was just another means to achieve the same ends, plunder.

When the Vikings built their long ship, there was nowhere to go but south. With little resistance at their first stop (a group of monks) and with great success there was little thought to not going back. With the build-up in frustration of not having and the feeling of battle boiling their blood, the Vikings needed to fight. They had sharpened their skills on each other; now others would feel the Viking might, and the Viking would discover what other races knew. Take what you can! Fighting is the right given to all whites though nature and / or religion. Bloodlust is the common thread that binds all white. The Vikings found that out when their bloodlust and arrogance met the passion of English steel. The so-called

Barbarians made Europe into a diverse people; Goths got so big that offspring took part of their name - the Visigoth - which would morph into the Spanish. Vikings became the modern-day Russians, Romans became Italian, while English and Vandals will start other European countries. While Egypt, Rome, and Greece educated the world, they would also unleash the bloodlust that whites brought out of Africa.

White has given the world everything that is now on the world's surface, all the good and the bad. The skin color change and the many changes the brain and body went through put whites on top. The only thing they had to fear was other whites. After a while, all white blended together. The only race other than white to conquer is the scourge of God – the Huns.

Huns. This group came out of the East to introduce the world to a new adjective: terror. The means that the Huns used had not been seen by the civilization of white rule, and the appearance of Huns enhanced their reputation as much as did their method of killing. Whites dealt with others that looked like them. The Hun, with long, dark, and unknown features shook the civilized world by their killing method, a style that stood out from anything that whites had ever seen.

As Rome trembled at the thought of being conquered by people that looked so unlike other enemies, God or nature stepped in to once again save whites. Attila the great leader died, as did the leader of the other great group of fighters from the east.

Mongols. Leader Genghis Khan, like the Vikings, lived in less-than-ideal conditions, and like the Vikings, the Mongol took from the group that was closest to his tribe. Resembling the Vikings, they demonstrated to the rest of the world their fighting skill. Their religion was to pray to nature. Huns, Mongols, and Vikings all shared similar religious beliefs, and only when it came to war did these seem to change.

The performance that all great leaders put on will play out the same with the same result. The great leader will conquer all that was conquered before him in the same brutal manner; at this point the man can only die. While a people with different skin tone is about to conquer white for the first time in the civilized world, God or Nature chose to save two races, the Chinese and white. Both were in sight of the great Khan, but Genghis Khan died, leaving behind Timur, or Tamerlane (A.D. 1336-1405), a Muslim Turco-Mongol ruler that became Iranized and conquered across Europe. Still, China was kept safe.

The only thing all this anarchy accomplishes is that the book on warfare grows thicker, as technique and tactics evolve. The problem never gets solved - how to share, how to keep peace, or how to solve conflict without use of the sword. When all races lose the leader that they depended on, they lose or give up their identity, and most chose to simply melt into wherever they happen to be at the time, a tendency that will inflict black as well.

White warfare will rage throughout the ages. One leader will replace another, and all will have the same success. All will overestimate their power and underestimate their knowledge of what people want and will tolerate. Education will play its part, and religion has a role. Religion will start to be important, then move to the background, and then emerge again. Every time it starts, white will be its champion, its protector. Throughout history, black will be the religious victim. While the white world moved forward, the black world only treads water, not gaining any traction, but not losing either, only standing still. Black waited to be used by all that needed the muscle, but not the mind - the body, but not the voice - the brain, but not the wisdom. Black was waiting for the entire world to get all that was, and white got all there was. Then black would give them more. Black was needed to keep white in the comfort they had grown accustomed to. The years of war could not go on forever, only just seem that way. There were constant breaks in the fighting, as the English, Spanish, French, and German had mostly split the world into pieces for themselves, so war was not as abundant.

Times changed, but greed and wonderment still coursed through the veins of all whites, and the open ocean called to all. Unlike black, she caused white to struggle, but white would ultimately prevail. The open ocean was the yellow brick road to white wealth.

As early man's body morphed into modern man's form, the hunter / gatherer's mind came along as well. The need to collect as much as possible took on new meaning as the modern human brain had conquered new ways of storing and growing. The new brain developed a new feature: jealousy. While this had no meaning to early humans, in modern man this trait developed in earnest. With the new addition of jealousy to the brain, something had to suffer, for the brain was still being filled with each generation. New additions meant something had to go or be curtailed, so the primitive human would still be part of the modern human, but placed in reserve.

Compassion was sacrificed, or at best, put away until really needed, as with the brutality inflected on native people. While early man felt the need to bury his dead and initiate a burial ritual, which could be the start of compassion, the end result was the need or desire to possess others' land and labor. Whereas white gain and hoarded wealth black was only getting by with nature as its master, black worked within the boundary of what nature provided or didn't provide. If there was meat, then blacks ate meat. If there were fish, blacks ate fish. If there was nothing, black moved to where there was something.

Wealth as white came to see it was meant to be controlled. White not only took and earned wealth, it actually made wealth: Gold.

Whereas native people used gold to adorn themselves, building idols to be prayed to, whites used gold to conquer what could not be taken. The descendants of the Visigoth needed all they could carry, and someone to carry it. The native that had gold would be put to the task of working the land that gold bought, but they will fail. The labor would prove to be too much for the body of the native to handle. So nature designed someone to handle the work as God had done with helping his chosen few. Religion gave reasons to release the native people from bondage, and this became the cause for others to take their place in bondage. The open ocean gave whites something to use their greatest gift against - the gift of wonderment. This gift allowed some blacks to leave Africa and forced whites to challenge the open and white world.

On the ocean great men discovered new land, and their ability to wage war made those lands fruitful, with all the nourishment of wealth for the taking. The trees were laid bare; the poor farmers were laid to rest where they fell. The ones left will bear witness to the absence of compassion. With Bible in hand the ocean-goer will claim all in the name of king and country. How can the phrase "Thou shall not kill" be overlooked? While spouting all the religion in the Bible (to people who did not understand), the conquistadors found passage to fill their need to enslave, destroy, and take what they wanted, the sword devoured its share. Disease did the rest, and the native spirit was broken. Compassion attempted to make amends for this treatment, but it would not be easy. Bishop Bartolomé de las Casas (A.D. 1484-1566), Dominican Friar and Spanish historian, let his compassion shine though, but only a little light, and it would not be shone on all. He championed the call for better treatment of the native Indians, aware that the work imposed by their European masters would break them beyond repair. For some, it was too little too late, but others only had to hold out for help to arrive.

The term *barbarian* will give Juan Ginés de Sepúlveda (A.D. 1494-1573), Spanish humanist and philospher, the means to fight against the bishop on behalf of Spanish colonialism. According to his theory, the barbarian worshipped idols, and this alone was reason to fight and confiscate all the natives possessed. The Bible clearly states that no one should worship idols, but this wasn't enough to continue to enslave people that were dying from disease and work. So the Bible must be used to make the point. Colonialists twisted biblical passages to convince the naysayer; wealth was at hand, and the wealth made only parts of the Bible important. Jose` de Acosta states: "Barbarians ignorant of Christian faith and literary culture are unfit for self-government; they can be considered "natura servi": fated by nature to serve, and civilized Christians should rule them.

This would not be enough to sway the Bishop from the bone he chose to chew. The enslavement of the native people could not be allowed to stand. He wrote to his Holy Father to take him to task in defense of the native people. With only a token show of support, the Bishop knew he just needed to replace the worker.

All manner of nations and religions have used slaves, the Muslim and the Christian. Yet, no nation or religion will perfect the owning of a people as the American white. With or without malice, the bishop will open the floodgates to the slave trade. With workers needed desperately, white will come back to visit the brother that was left behind centuries earlier. It will not be a happy family reunion. Germany, Portugal, England, France, Arabia, and the

Dutch all will benefit from the slave trade. The Americas will also benefit, but all will pale in comparison to the ills of white.

Black could, where natives could not work effectively in the tropical heat. Black could, where natives had a religious champion (black did not, not in the places they were sent). Nature and religion can be seen as the fate that Jose` Acosta wrote of. Blacks have been the servant since their founding by whites. Never in black history have blacks been the holder of servants whose skin did not reflect their own. The wealth that white held will come from the ground, from the body, and all points in between. White will mix the earth's minerals to make wealth - bronze comparison to North America. Ghana, Nigeria, Tanzania, and parts of interior and sub-Sahara Africa will send millions of bodies across the ocean. Not all millions will be stolen, but millions will arrive, and not all that arrive will stay. All will be treated differently, all will be broken, some will stay broken, others will be remade, and all will be lost.

The beginning of the fading black race has been evolving over many centuries or even millennia. Old Testament Ham was cursed, not by God, not by God's will, but by the will of his father, the beginning of servitude as it relates to black and religion. Nature did not see fit to give black the treasure of wonderment. Nature did give black the strength to persevere. Where the native people could not fight off iron and steel weapons and armor, white will use plants to make wealth, and white will connect the whip to black skin to make a country.

With religion as their guide and greed as their logic, the making of America began. In 1492, Columbus sailed the ocean blue - so what! Columbus landed in the Caribbean, but the real treasure was the Quaker lands in North America. It was then that Europe was experiencing the first sexual revolution. Centuries of war had boiled down to the haves and the want-to-gets. Without constant warfare, peace had to be replaced with something, and the something was sex! The church was trying to control sex, but did not have a good idea how. The king was to answer to the church, and the church was to answer to the king, but sex answered to no one. The faithful was surrounded by debauchery and wanted some religion that they could control. The Quaker wanted to practice what was not being practiced in England. They would go to the New World, the one that was to become America. In the New World fortune could be found, taken, and grown. The growing would call for labor. The labor would be too harsh for some; the wealth would make it too hard for the wealthy. Someone would have to do the work. This quest for labor would in itself create wealth, and slaves were needed. Not just any slave, slaves that could stand the long hours and the heat, and not cost much to keep. The need was for an animal that could think and reason, an animal that could reproduce offspring to replace the parent. Black was the answer.

What is slavery? Drudgery, the owning of slaves as a practice.

What is a slave? A human being who is owned as property by another. Simply put, a slave is property, and slavery is work done by the slave.

Work. As a concept, work is all that slavery was, no matter how hard, no matter how degrading, it was only work, just work. So why is slavery so taboo, a topic not to discuss in mixed company? Was it the fact that black worked under hazardous conditions? No. Black to this day work in jobs that are hazardous. Could it be black worked for no pay? No. blacks were given free room and board, medical treatment, the same as black prisoners today. Could it be that black was taken from their homes? No. blacks have been captive in wars for centuries, also like black prisoners of today.

Then why is slavery such a hot topic to discuss?

One reason (of many) is the skin color of some blacks, or the skin color that some blacks have - the light-skinned black.

The second reason was while slavery was harsh, it was the manner of getting the worker to the job that was the first of many indignities visited on black. The total lack of compassion in the shipping of blacks could only prove the diminishing compassion in whites. To pack anything in its own fecal matter and the fecal matter of others is barbarism at its worst. But the owner simply placed the order; he didn't ship black - he was only there to receive what he had paid for. The fact that white showed no consideration for black's plight proved the slow growth of white apathy toward black life.

Savages. Seeing the half-dressed dark skin was the only thing that came to the minds of white. What if black did dress appropriately? What then? What if black plight was simply the fact that they couldn't afford the right clothing? The fact that the clothes could be the beginning of the downfall of black is a consideration to be made. Look at the clothing of black today: young black. Would it have stopped black from becoming slave? Doubtful. The clothing could only slightly cover up the black skin. The Bible and nature would do the rest.

Rice was found in some areas of Africa. Cotton was found in some areas of Africa. The color blue was found in some areas of Africa (at least the means to make blue). White was found in some areas of Africa. The knowledge to grow and export these products was found in some areas of Africa. Why weren't these products grown and shipped from Africa? Why was there a need for slaves? Why was there a need for shipment of people?

Chapter 3

From Slave to Soldier

From the days of Adam and Eve to the era of Lucy and Ardi, black skin has been
on a path to slavery. America will be the road, filled with potholes, cracks, and ultimately,
redemption.

Who is smarter - white or other skin colors?

White.

In 1492, white Europeans found or discovered native people in the western
hemisphere and gave them a name, a name some use to this day: Indian. This designation
came from a mistake. The explorer wasn't where he thought he was and misnamed the native
inhabitants of the Americas, but the name stuck and became the erroneous identity of a
people that will forever be marginalized. The carnage that followed the Europeans' assault of
the native inhabitants was death of a race, by weapons, religion and disease. Sickness,
religion, and nature all will play a part in the coming of black to America.

In the early history of slavery, it was mostly as servant. People caught during war
by warriors enslaved the loser, the loser now had a debt to pay. The early slaves were more
like employees than what a slave in America would become. The wealth of crops such rice
and cotton would increase the need for labor, so this increased the number of slaves that were
needed.

In early American history it was just work. Wealth meant power. "Absolute power
will corrupt absolutely," as the saying goes. Work gave way to cruel and very usual
punishment. Native people were to be the workers but southern native people were basically

allergic to white. Native people died off because they were allergic to their masters. Nature made sure they were not able to perform the required tasks in the heat and harsh conditions. Not only were they not suited to withstand this type of repression, but nature gave them no cure to combat the insect bite, the mosquito in particular. The mosquito could cause malaria. Nature had a cure, but didn't see fit to give it to all. The cure: sickle cell. The cure will be nature's gift to white in the body of black. The cure will come after slavery and hold on to black. The cure will not be needed after slavery, but not taken back by nature. While white was going through various incarnations and using his love of curiosity to build a civilization, blacks were developing genes to become slaves. Mosquitos were killing Africans at a high rate sometime in the past, and nature's answer was to give black a gene defect - not the ability to build nets, or housing, or medicine to fight malaria, just a defective gene.

High blood pressure was another condition given to black, a need that would buy black time to get across an ocean. Low intelligence was another gift or punishment for not keeping pace with white civilization. Nature gave black all the accoutrements that would be needed to be slaves. In the 1600's slaves embarked on the twisted journey of being black in America. As slaves gathered in their master's quarters, the thought of what, why, and how gave way to work, work here, work hard, work now. White in America gave new meaning to the terms *slave owner* and *master*. White will attempt to conquer what has never been conquered before, and nearly, very nearly, accomplish it, the complete ownership of a person.

The Egyptians had slaves, the Romans had slaves, the Greeks had slaves, and all three had soldiers that were willing to fight and die for the causes of their leadership. They would be soldiers first, but their loyalty was flexible. Some would be loyal to the crown;

others would be loyal to a person. But neither crown nor person held onto soldiers and slaves as the Americans held onto the black slave. No one but the white in America so completely owned a race. As slavery went, the American experience was and still is the gold standard. The black slave in America has been well documented; the effect of it has been seen and documented, but not so completely.

The long-term effect has not been adequately evaluated. This is where white has been the most effective. The slave owner not only amassed great wealth on the back of blacks, but also put in place the need for black to aspire to be one with white. American white gave black a curse or a tiny hypnotic suggestion: Who am I?

Black tried to hold on to Africa, some at the cost of their life; all paid the price of African pride. But the only pride white would allow was the pride in a job well done. So who was black? The first generation to be born in America will be inflicted with this sickness. No home, little to any leadership, nothing to make one stand out from the other. White took black history and replaced it with his own history. White took black pride and buried it under millions of pounds of cotton, rice, and tobacco.

The Africans that made the first ocean voyage were black African. The ones that were born in America were nothing. They weren't people; some weren't blood relatives - they were only a group of workers. Black also noticed the change in skin color; their children's skin was being lightened. This is where "who am I" really shocks the system of black. With no history to bond to, blacks leaned on each other. Knowingly or unknowingly white starts to take the only thing that held the race together, the common bond of black skin. When black was afflicted with the white gene, the need to want came with it, and blacks' movements from one another would follow.

From their life on the savannahs of Africa, blacks had not progressed as whites had. The struggle that influenced the growth of white didn't exist in Africa. Weather, food, and shelter, as meager as it may have been, worked for the African. The need to want just for the sake of having did not readily infect Africans; not until black encounters with white did the need-to-want gene manifest in the masses of black. White through deed only showed black that having things meant power and privilege. The knowledge of *want* will corrupt the soul of black. The ease of white life or what is perceived as easy, would send black on the road to his demise. Black will not go quietly into that good night, not at first. He will struggle though slavery, fighting with the call to freedom; he will fight the rage of family rape, and he will fight the selling of his family. He will endure white greed. While black toils in fields, white taints his family gene pool. Black had only the family white allowed him. Black was responsible for all children, his and white: The children whites had in their household and the children of whites in black households. Slavery took more than the life and strength of black - it took the pride of the man. Black ease of adaptability was the key to the molding of black; black could be made to father and abandon children, children that were used as currency by white. This ease of abandonment will follow black into the centuries that follow. The father that is forced to see the child of another man at the table of his making and not having the ability to right the wrong feels his manhood being eroded.

The fact that white can lord over the house of black also affects the woman. The black woman will grow to misuse the black man. While some will be the victim of black, others will be the victor.

All slavery and slaves were not created equal. Some black became slave owners themselves; other succeeded in other ways. The history of slavery did not end with the

Emancipation Proclamation, nor the Civil War. The end to slavery as an open society ended, but slavery will never end for black; the effects of slavery for black will perhaps follow white and black to the end of time. Slavery and its effect can be seen in the face of all blacks, be it dark skin or light. The rape that produces light skin and the sea voyage that carried black is always present. The struggle black has today is the truth that slavery lives and so do white and war.

The revolution: "We hold these truths to be self-evident, that all men are created equal..." This is the foundation of the U.S. Declaration of Independence; it is the creation of white in America.

Its seeds were planted by black, harvested by black, and rewarded to white. The Declaration was due to the good fortune of the thirteen original colonies and the slave labor that produced it.

As the overseer of the colonies, English rule failed to heed history's warning. The history of civilization had shown that people must be respected. The fall of all the countries with whom England had a common interest resulted from failure in the treatment of its people, and the citizens sometimes failed the leaders.

The wars that the English fought did little to prepare them for the war with white America. America had done what very few countries dared. With little to no major war experience, America was willing to gamble on colonists' willingness to fight for their homeland. The French would be on standby, entering only after seeing that America was worthy of support. Black slaves had only to swear allegiance to the crown and be free. Blacks split; some went over to the British, while others willingly fought and risked captured. Why? Why would black be willing to fight and die against certain freedom?

"We hold these truths to be self-evident, that all men are created equal."

These words gave black all the reason they would need to fight. While life in England could be paradise for blacks, black didn't know England, black knew America, the early America - not the America that it would become, Black didn't know the meaning of life outside of white-life. Some blacks chose what they knew.

Others took the chance that England would give what America had not: self-pride. "All men are created equal" would be the phrase, the key to unlock the door of future rights for black. That door would stay locked for centuries, but blacks would keep the key and pass it along to their future selves. Why at a time of slavery would white put these words on paper for all to see? Could this have been the key that some white forefather left for future black to use?

Not all white, even at this early date of slavery, were for slavery. Not all wanted to be brushed with this paint. While the founding fathers had slaves, not all was in favor of continuing the practice. Could this be their way of forcing future whites to deal with what they did not want to deal with? The landing of the first white on Plymouth Rock in 1620 meant that they could rule themselves, pay homage to their king, but be the leader of their own destiny - or so they thought.

First, white needed the help of the Native people to keep from starving or freezing to death. Unlike Columbus and his crew the English came gently ashore. They allowed the Natives to help, without killing them off through disease; the killing would come later. They needed to send money back to their king. The speed at which the colonies became united and stately hastens the need-versus-the want factor. While the homeland was waiting for taxes or failure from the colonies, the colonies were becoming a superpower. They were learning from the Native; they were building up their slave population and no longer looking to the homeland to give them anything, as they were more concerned about what the homeland was taking.

The child that had crossed the ocean became a rebellious teen:

When in the course of human events it becomes necessary for one people to dissolve the political bands which have connected them with another, and to assume among the powers of the earth, the separate and equal station to which the laws of nature and of nature's God entitle them, a decent respect to the opinions of mankind requires that they should declare the cause which impels them to the separation.

Translation: White would no longer be the obedient children that crossed the ocean 150+ years earlier. White had grown, and they could feed and clothe themselves, so they were free to make their own decision. They decided to leave the old world behind, all of which led to their picking a fight – and they did.

The Paul Revere illustration of the Boston Massacre and the commentary that went along with it (the first use of cinematic brain washing) anti-tax protest, the Boston tea party, and small attacks in and around Massachusetts meant that the American Revolution was at hand and black would be there, at least the few that were given or who took the chance to fight.

In 1787 South Africa fought war as little more than a heated argument. Nature would give southern Africa a glimpse into what white had been up to since their evolutionary leap out of Africa millions of years before. Shaka Zulu: with his birth South Africa bore witness to carnage. For the first time a Black man would rival White. For the first time(not the last time/black on black death) black would spill blood on a massive scale, all for payment: Payment for lack of respect, for indignity. Shaka's mother was used by a man, or she used a man. The end result was a man without guidance, a boy filled with rage and the means to exact his vengeance. Shaka would have to wait for his chance to repair his mother's broken past, but his waiting would only simmer and bring to a boil his need or lust for revenge. When his opportunity did arrive, the spigot opened and blood flowed. With the blood loss came a unified South Africa, but it was built on a faulty model, on the model of the old European style of pain for glory. Do what you are told and receive no pain. Praise your king so he feels might in your glory to him. The pain and glory technique only lead to his demise, in the style of the Roman, death by family. This gift of nature showed what black was capable of in war; what was not known by blacks was how far behind they were in putting these techniques in practice. In this case what you don't know can kill you, and will! From the day white landed on Plymouth Rock, black had been only a tool. The fact that black could think meant he was a tool that could not just be put away when not needed. So there were conflicts in what to do with the tool that thinks. War would deepen this conflict. What to do with the black tool? Cannot let him sit idly by while white fought and died. White didn't want black to be soldiers in their army. To do so would be to say black was considered a man of equal standing. Right?

A British garrison being harassed by citizens in Boston formed a line and prepared to fire; the first shot found a mulatto man named Crispus Attucks. Black finds it noteworthy to say the first man to die in the battle for independence was black, but he was most likely of mixed race. Should this diminish black thinking? Yes. Because the white nature of him put him in white company. A black man on the street of Boston with only white, and he's at ease with them? At ease enough to taunt British soldiers? How many blacks at that time could have done what he had? The fact that white memorialized this event as a black man dying at the hand of the British is a testament to how some whites were conflicted as to the status of black. Attucks may have been a runaway slave. What does this say about the thought process of black? It may show how the conflict in white is showing up in black as well.

In 1775 the battle for America's independence began. In 1775 the battle for equality began. The war for America's independence would be fought on America's soil; the battle for the rights of black would be fought in the minds of Americans. The separation of blacks from each other was fought in the soul of black America. While slave owners that didn't want to fight or could not fight sent slaves in their place, the general consensus was black would be excluded from fighting. The British would use this to their advantage. The war would give some blacks an escape route. The boats used to bring black to America would give black a position to fight from. The use of blacks on ship was not as frowned upon as using blacks on land. This was something that would bind black and white together like a spring, tight in a crisis, pulled apart afterward, only to be brought together time and again (WHITE POWER). The thought of black on land with guns was not an appealing choice to the slave owner. While the British offered freedom, the Americans offered death - and not just any death, the vilest form of death - hanging. Hanging as it relates to military life - lynching for the common man or mob. With the threat of such a death one would think that black would just stay and watch and wait for the outcome. This would not be the case; black would leave the torment of slavery for death or the British line, and while some chose to fight, still others went to find a plot of land to call their own, a plot to live on or be buried in.

White had to fight the British as well as keep a lookout for their farms and runaway slaves. The slave issue and the war were parallel; one had little precedent over the other.

Runaway slaves were hunted and used as weapons. The runaway slave had little chance of being anything other than fodder for white, and white gained a useful purpose for runaways; if the British were going to give them refuge, then the Americans were going to give the slave a parting gift: Smallpox - the start of germ warfare in the New World.

Smallpox was given to slaves; the slaves were then allowed to go to the British, where all that came in contact with the runaway were infected. White entrance to the New World was another leap forward for white, their next evolutionary step. They had learned a lesson from history others had failed to heed. While treating blacks as servant and slaves, white also allowed blacks to learn, not with forethought just by black being in close proximity. Black learned the offer of the British; black learned that not all white wanted to fight. Black learned ways of becoming free, becoming soldiers. As in all warfare, battles were won and lost; with their losses the Americans did what they had done from the start, turn to black. While some individuals could not stomach black with weapons, all was reminded of the big picture, "If we don't all hang together we will surely all hang" by Benjamin Franklin. This gave black its most important bit of knowledge. Have skin in the game; if black were ever to get any respect, he had to have some skin in the game. The only logical conclusion to not wanting black to fight was the hope of not giving them any fire power, be it weapon or skin. White needed to keep black at arm's length; black could assist the white soldier, cook or clean, but given the chance to fight, only then could he learn his true value. He could earn his place at the table of America, but this would not happen quickly.

The future Americans had defeated the British before the revolution began. How? They were firstly fighting for themselves, not for a king; the future Americans were fighting on their own soil. The future Americans were fighting with all they had, and what the future Americans had were black, native, and a sense of destiny. What the English had was conceit, and their conceit made them unwilling to change their style of fighting. The English also had a disdain of the French from earlier wars.

This conceit would find its way to the colonies, and the result will be another family feud.

Yes, slavery was wrong, but it was work. Making white rich with little to no compensation was wrong, but that also meant someday you could be sent somewhere to be free, your land or your death. But to assist in the fighting, to assist in the winning, to assist in the building of America, to be a soldier was to say to white "I am willing!" "No matter the cost, I am willing!" That level of commitment would only be overlooked for a century or so.

Arm black - don't arm black.

Use the slave - don't use the slave.

You will be FREE - you won't be free.

Stay in America - go with the British.

Black was bombarded with thoughts, with options, with do's and don'ts. Some chose wisely, while others had the choice made for them. Some fought, some watched, all learned. Some learned more than others; this would set the footing for black to distrust white and other black.

The British with centuries of warfare on their side were soundly defeated by the upstart colonies. America was on the super highway to becoming a super power. Black was on its way to becoming convicts.

After the war some blacks gained their freedom, some took their freedom, other didn't fare so well. Black was sent back to field and farm; some found themselves sold down the river, sold onto islands of sugar plantation. The British took some, but didn't give all that was advertised. The mistrust of white began in earnest.

While black knew his place as a slave, to have been a soldier built a sense of pride into his blackness - to be educated in military ways and discipline, and the thrill of open combat. The willingness of a man to die for a man was black America that would come, but for most it will be like tomorrow is always coming, just only be on call today. "Tomorrow we will be free, but not today." Blacks went back to being nothing! This was hard to swallow, but not impossible. Black went back to slave life, only now with pride. Black had his taste of progress. His eyes had seen the greatness of what America had to offer, and black knew the path his offspring would travel. Soon.

While America dealt slowly with the issue of slavery, blacks were gaining their independence. Black was learning the rules of life in America, and the rule was money. After the revolution: Black starts to read, buys his freedom, buys land, and buys slaves of his own. Free blacks live and work side by side with enslaved blacks; the crab-in-a-bucket effect begins in the minds of BLACK - an effect that could have been coincidental? The crab effect is one crab constant pulling and crawling over the other to gain ground, to leave the bucket.

With America's victory the nation was introduced to humility, humility in the form of George Washington, the general that won America's independence the general that would become America's first president. Not all Americans wanted to be done with men wearing crowns; some wanted Washington to be king, and George Washington could have easily become king, but he chose to be president. The humility of George Washington kept America with only a few pressing problem, he would not be one. George Washington had the foresight to not go into the business of owning an empire. The insight of the first president would be an opening for future black. The humility he showed did as much for America as did winning the war. Would this be the luck or the destiny of America? Washington was only the first president, but he would show the world America in the flesh. Washington will be America: compassionate and conflicted.

Washington's ability to turn enemies into friends, friends into the labor force, and a dark day into a bright future would be America's ability, also. George Washington was not born into privilege. At a very young age George Washington learned pain, the destruction of his boyhood home by fire, the death of his father, events that forced him to grow up sooner than most boys of his age. The same could be said of America: the pilgrim also had a trial by fire, and was also forced to grow up quickly and to build the thirteen colonies quickly. America the young nation had to contend with her native people, while seeming to allow the native to make room for her conqueror. George Washington at the age of eleven was a slave owner; it would take his lifetime to come to an outward understanding of what could be called an immoral act. He always knew that slavery was wrong, but only expressed the fact after he could no longer benefit from their labor. Several trips to death's door were taken by George Washington, all with a return trip: fire at his boyhood home, blotched attempt by a native to shoot a twenty-something Washington, the fall into an icy river and the freezing of the same river so he could walk across it, and a battle in the French and Indian War where nearly all the officers died, with the exception of Washington. Washington had several bullet holes in his clothing, but none in him. These events were the first coating of Teflon for white's great character. Although Washington and America were out-gunned and out-fought, still America and Washington would be victorious. Destiny or British arrogance?

Black and war: The question that white had about black would appear time and again. First - will black fight?

Second - can they learn?

Third - and the greater question spoken in private - will black kill white?

War! White in America was getting good at battle; the war of 1812 would give the whites in America a chance to be tested in a naval battle, and who better than the British to test itself? They had defeated their enemies on land, and now the sea would bear witness to the might of America. Still, black would fight for the British and the American. Still, only a few black would face freedom, some by the British, and more by the American. Still others would run away. After yet another victory the slave issue stayed the same. Some whites said yes to freedom; other said no. Money speaks for some. No matter how one thought of slavery, it was a money-maker. Heart speaks for others - the one that had little to no vested interest in slavery, the northerner. Black had only themselves and no other. Native people had land and family, tradition and culture; they welcomed the immigrants, helped them through the first few years, gave them knowledge and security. They were paid back with sickness, war, and death. Why, then, didn't black and Native not combine forces? White might? Or a place in the pecking order of white's world. "I'm called a red savage, but I'm not a black slave."

The first consideration is white's complete assassins of black character, and how white without trying gained the respect of the people they had fought and would continue to fight until they had the entirety of gifts that the native's land could give. Still it was better than being black. Why?

The war of 1812 was fought not for freedom, but money. The war of 1812 was in some ways unnecessary, but it gave America the motive to put an army together. The young nation put ships to sea, built its first special operations force to test in battle, a battle that was only American. The conclusion of the War for Independence and the War of 1812 was the courtship for America. War would be her mate, and she would conceive and give birth to twins: compassion and conflict. And the young country would add a soundtrack to her name. "The Star-Spangled Banner" and it would become the most famous song and cloth besides the Shroud of Turin. The American flag and anthem would represent America as both compassionate and conflicted. As a young nation with a victorious thirteen colonies, America would need more. Thirteen states were not enough. America needed land, and white wanted to grow.

Manifest destiny: This proclamation meant certain death for native people; it meant that all the land would become America, and they would live in America, and America would take care of them in one way or the other. White would own land from sea to sea. And all will fight or fall to keep it.

The Mexican and American War: As the native people had done earlier, the Mexican gave in to the advances of white. This allowed the whites to set up homes in what would become Texas and had been part of Spain and France, but only flourished as America. The Mexican would not give in to white, nor allow them to make the rules. Mexicans felt that whites, as guests, should follow and not lead. The question of slavery would again prove that America had to come to some sort of compromise.

"Remember the Alamo!" These words added to the superpower that America was to become. The Alamo became the tomb of what it meant to be an American, the fight to the end. The battle wasn't winnable; it was the means to an end. It was the engine to prime the pump of battle. When America needs something, something to get things going, someone has to be sacrificed; the American Revolution, the Boston Massacre, the war of 1812; no death means no meaningful resolution. The Civil War, attack on fort Sumter, and so on.

The Mexican and American War wasn't meaningful until "Remember the Alamo." The slave question not only caused a war, but as luck would have it, it added to the size of America. More luck or more destinies?

Size will matter in the oil boom to come. Although Mexicans wanted no slaves in what was Mexico, black still fought for America. Why? Ownership, skin in the game. From the 1600's to the 1800's white not only enslaved black bodies but enslaved black mind and black image. Native people owned slaves to become more white-like. Natives adopted white dress and mannerisms to be more white-like. Natives betrayed each other to be more white-like. All the pain and suffering, all the broken promises - anything was better than pairing with black. In the preceding 200 years, black had been reduced to the mindset of a battered wife or an abused child. The black mind was pushed by the thought of freedom and pulled by the reality of white indifference. Black must have prayed and held out hope that the sermon and biblical readings they heard were also meant for them as well as whites; some took the Bible verses to mean that killing was for all.

Nat Turner shook the foundation of white life when he took the Bible of whites and put it into practice. Not only will white be judge and jury, but the Bible meant he, too, could be the bringer of death. And he was. Nat Turner gave white fear no war had - the fear that black was in their midst, and some wanted out. The con game that was pushed on other whites was shown to be not as true as white had thought. The con that said black was happy with his station in life was turned on its head in 1831. Armed blacks went on the rampage. Looking back, why was a black rebellion so feared by white? The worst thing that could happen was the closest white would die. This would be terrible if the white were you, but not as horrific as having white's country taken. Why, then, was Nat Turner's quest so feared? Could it have been not the deed but the thought? The thought that one day white would serve black? The thing that worked against Nat Turner was black skin. Where to hide among white? From the first boatload of blacks to set foot on American soil, the same had been true. No hiding black skin in a sea of white, the rebellion was doomed from the start; slaves armed with hoes (farm utensil): picks; knives; and shovels were no match for guns, years of fighting, and a sea of white skin. Their capture was assured, as assured as the black skin on their backs. The consequences of their actions would be met with savagery of its own. With the smell of blood in the air, white would reap their vengeance with the blood of the guilty and innocent alike. The Nat Turner rebellion was put down as bloodied as it had started, and then a little extra for others thinking of trying the same thing. The rebellion was seen as the most horrible thing one human could do to another, but the response was seen as an adequate reaction, or compassion and conflict. The greatest thing to come from Nat Turner's rebellion was another battle in the fight for slaves' freedom. With each victory and defeat Americans came closer to resolving the issue of slavery, which is why black fought. The prize for competing would one day be freedom. The wars that America fights would in time split America into two separate, but equal, identities. Arrogance and compassion, the twins, would push and pull America in and out of war and peace. Arrogance and compassion, and compassion and conflict, will and have been the definition of war in America. The fact that America shows compassion to even her enemies gives the viewer pause to say that the atrocities America commits are justified. But the conflict is what has made America great. Only a great country will not rush into armed conflict just because a friend is in peril. The arrogance is the part that makes America a villain in the eyes of the viewer.

The first push would be the civil war; arrogance would take the place of conflict. The conflict was over; the conflict was what to do with black. Arrogance took its place. Arrogance claimed the position it knew best - what is best for the black Southerner, and what is best for the nation. Compassion used the position that all was well. Black needed to be taken care of and whites need workers and need to be taken care of; black was going to do it, and no one would make it not be so. Both believed their position to be the right one - so much so that they would go to war over it. The Civil War would pit one family against the other. Brother against brother. Father against son. Blood from all. The War Between the States showed that America would be righteous; America would spill the blood of the unrighteous. America determined what is meant by the term *righteous*, and America would also change the meaning of the term as it saw fit. The battle for the right to be right will change America, partly for the better, but partly for the worst.

As in earlier wars, black was given the right to fight, and at this point that's what it is - a right. Arming blacks after what Nat Turner's raid did to the psychology of whites was a gamble, one that would only be taken after the war was seen to be faltering, again. Black as before showed that they could and were willing to fight for what was the country of their birth. The country, with this war, could one day be called home. While black units did not immediately gain the respect of the white units, they would only need time. Battle would give whites a reason to respect blacks, if not the man, at least the man's performance. When there was a task not worthy of white death, black was sent in to hold the line or advance the line. The 16th president would at last give black the reward that earlier presidents could not: Freedom.

The Civil War. This war would show the world that America was not just America, but the United States of America, no matter the different colors, no matter the different opinions; through blood and pain America would unite, eventually. And as the United States of America they would live together even if it meant killing some to make it happen. Brother fought against brother, father against son, all right, all willing to die to prove to the other their point of view is wrong. Only after a large number of people have died will the War Between the States cease. Black would bear witness to the need for white to control all in their view. Only after severe losses would the great emancipator find the courage to do what his predecessor had set the groundwork for someone else to do. Black after countless victories fails to learn what it meant to be American.

Some learned that it is the fight that America respects. Some felt that it is the never-give-up attitude that gains favor. Still others felt that it was the fight against others that makes America great, and makes one an American, but this changes as does the ocean tide. Blacks have been searching for what it means to be an American but have yet to find the American Holy Grail. This is a lesson black cannot learn because it is for white only, the rule maker and breaker.

"Freedom is a road seldom traveled by the multitude."

"Freedom is the absence of having nothing left to lose."

Freedom. These great quotes loom large in the practice of being free, as it relates to the freeing of two hundred years of servitude. For the first time in black history the black man and woman were free. They were free from the bondage of his hunter's gathering mind. He was free from the nomadic lifestyle. He was free from the use of the whip. He was free from the security of his master's farm. He was free from the only home he knew. He was free to be nothing. He was free to be something. He was on his own. Freedom points to roads seldom traveled by the multitude. The multitude now included what black had been free to become: The multitude of homeless, the multitude of the unemployed, the multitude of the uneducated, the multitude of potential, the potential to be taken advantage of, the potential to be killed, the potential to grow and help to grow America. Black had a clean slate, slightly clean. A slate that would hold the entire picture that black will draw. Black will be all things that America has to offer. Black will become a slave to his mind. Free from the bonds of white, black will enslave himself. Not so much his body, but his most prized possession, his mind, all in the effort to look for the answer to the question white had planted in his mind: WHO AM I? Black will find that freedom isn't what he hopes it would be.

BANG! The death of the great emancipator and white power was used as a tool of death. The white man lay in wait for the first blow to the black man's newfound pride and his first step toward apathy from white.

After years of fighting for the white man's country, the black man now was fighting for self-pride, self-recognition, something that said, "Job well done." After centuries of free labor with only minor flare-ups, the Black man needed to hear, "You have done America proud." But what the Black man got was the death of the great emancipator. While in bondage the country was growing: natives went through the trail of tears, Mexicans fought and died to give up Texas, Lewis and Clark along with a native girl and a black slave carved maps through the Louisiana Purchase. The Homestead Act gave free land to all that could claim and hold it. The Black man being free got only freedom - and Jim Crow. While other immigrants came to get free land, the Black man got segregation and discrimination. The Black man was free to not mix with white, although white would not have the same problem, mixing with black women and some men. Black could cook, clean, and rear white children, but not be sworn in using the same Bible as white. With the number of mulatto children clearly seen, no Constitutional amendment was called for; the children were not to be spoken of. The taint of white blood would bring peace and scorn to the recipient. While black skin was a disdain to white eyes, he wasn't the only victim, nor was native or Mexican.

Hawaii. Religion once again comes to the aid of white. The Hawaiian island was discovered, just like America was discovered. Goodbye to self-rule, hello to missionaries coming to give the good Word and take possession of the island. Without firing a shot America got bigger. The self-rule of a separate nation was dissolved with fear and intimidation, again: Those absent of white's religion must be ruled by white. The lack of clothes and dark skin color is a moot point? Right.

All was done so white could have more: More land, more control, more money, more need to get more and an advantage to better wage war. While black struggled to get his feet under him, other races came to America with its offer of free land. The means to keep the land was promised by the legal system, but the legal system that would do more to harm black than to help him. If Black gets a piece of land, there's no seeds; he get seeds, there's no equipment; he gets equipment, it comes with so much debt that he can never seem to break even. His counterpart, new white immigrant, not only gets, but prospers. Black must fight nature and white just to break even. Free blacks have struggled from both ends; his wife sees the treatment white gives him with no recourse. He sees how his wife looks at him and the treatment he endures. The years of slavery to free men will at last give black the time to study who he is; this time will show black he isn't anybody. To his wife he is a man, but more of a male than a man. To himself he is not a man; he is only a male. The need to become a man will haunt him and all his descendants. The only thing that makes him seem manly is military service to his country. To be a soldier is his only comfort, but he can't hide there forever. Black willingness to fight will be called on again and again, but years will go by before equality is established. With the power of life and death hovering over the head of black, white felt more empowered. The power was shown in the number of mulatto children born to black women of all age group.

Absolute power corrupts absolutely. Power over a person is an intoxication that white will pass down through his family tree. The ability to rape with no thought to punishment will wither the family tree of black. The removal of mix-race children from the sight of the white woman will cause an upheaval in the black family tree. Why would the white woman put up with the rape of another woman? Why would the white woman put up with the infidelity of the white man? In most cases she did because the white woman had married for money and power; love would come later if the white woman didn't allow sex to cripple her or her family. White would marry cousins in a bid to keep land and money under one family name. Black, on the other hand, could only be what white allowed them to be. When white first learned to kill in the conflict of war, he learned to respect the warrior, no matter how costly the battle. The fight was what counted. This was the beginning of the Empathic Movement of white against black. From the American Revolution to Afghanistan, black has earned white admiration, an admiration that fades soon after the bullets cease. Why? The *why* is always the American conflict, the conflict that stymied black people. The why is this: there was no black and white war. Without this there is a perception that black has been given the American experience. Why? Not all whites saw the treatment black skin had to endure. Not all whites thought of slavery from the black viewpoint. Since all races experience some form of slavery, they only had their view of what slavery was, and to some it was only work. What cannot be expressed is the totality of the black slave experience - slavery was just work, but the institution of slavery was something else. Slavery from white's view is through a war lens:

Fight.

Die.

Get captured.

Become a slave.

Fight your way out of your circumstance. Fight or die. Live in slavery or die. This is the thought of a race of warriors. To live in a constant state of war is to understand battle, but this also breeds contempt of those who do not know battle. Before Shaka Zulu, battle and war were nothing to blacks. From ancient Egypt in non-biblical history to the exodus in biblical history, white has had a continual history of war.

Respect and empathy have been measured by the warrior code. For hyphenated Americans, the black struggle is of their own making. It is difficult to express to a German why your struggle is reason to give to you; a cold weather warrior like the German means to fight or die. In the fight that gave black his manhood, the Civil War led to the Irish rioting; they did not want to fight for the right of a people that should fight for themselves. They did not want to fight for the same people they would be fighting for jobs with. The fighting spirit that black men fought with, side by side with white men, should have been the same spirit they fought side by side with other black men with.

The failure was that they were always surrounded. There was no blending in to the crowd, as with German fighting Russian, or Spanish soldier fighting the Mexican soldier. Black was black, and to get the respect that he was giving to white he needed war. The Revolutionary War was his birth. The Civil War was his evolutionary leap from child to teen; the wars in between and after were merely a tune-up for the black foray into adulthood. In 1917 black got a glimpse into white's past - global war! In World War I, black saw what white was and was capable of. Global war showed black what white was willing to do, and how they were willing to do it. Poison gas, germ warfare, mass killing - all for the right to be right. Another generation of black would have to face the ongoing theme of what to do with black, black that wanted to build a country, that on paper was to be a country for all, but what black will find out is that paper does not win heart and minds, a lesson that has been long and tedious on blacks. Blacks learned or relearned that not all whites would treat them the same; some European whites could be viewed as honorable related to battle. This would only be truly evident in the Second World War. This is where black blood, the blood in centuries of American conflicts, will finally rest. For centuries black blood was wasted on white war with little to show for the men and the family of men that shed it, lacking great recognition during and tepid recognition after, if at all. But after World War II, black's blood would finally rest in peace, a peace that will require others to fulfill its wish. This was the wish for freedom, the wish long denied, but long sought. World War II brought black into manhood. After December 7, 1941, white was rudely awakened to the sound of America's heart beating.

Attack!

The Japanese bombing of Pearl Harbor sent chills throughout America; the peace and quiet of faraway battle had come noisily home. This would be the test, and the last time black would ask for the privilege to serve. Now war made progress; no longer was America hiding in trees, changing the rules of civilized warfare. Now the entire rulebook was being written and re-written. America had the money, but did not have the war knowledge of seasoned warriors. This would soon change, and the reason was the melting pot effect. America was fighting the Japanese, some of which were residing in this country. They also fought Germans, some of which the country would become. Then there were Italians, which most of the country was mixed with. They were a match for America but not for the offspring of the young that would call themselves American. Black would once again fight through the setback of his skin color, and white would fight through the problem of what to do with black. The answer was and always has been to let them fight. Only this time - this time - black will be asked. Black will lead not just black, but all, after the war ends.

In 1948, the death of Franklin D. Roosevelt gave President Truman the keys to power, and he used them to unlock the binds on blacks in the military. Through trial and error, through mistrust and deed, through force and treachery, through rain, sleet, and snow the black man has never failed to shine; he has gleamed through slave chains, lynch mobs, just and unjust accusations, and finally after the world fought its second global war did white allow him to be a solider, a soldier with all rights and privileges. Black had arrived, at least for a while.

After World War II, black came back to America; he was a new black - he was becoming a person of color. While not all white respected the skin of the black man, some respected the uniform of the soldier. There were others that respected the fight of the black solider. Still others respected the whole man.

The black woman after World War II for the first time had a man. The black woman had a man that could take care of her in all ways. She had an educated man, a man with his head held high, and a man that knew the ways of white life, a man that could live like white and not give up his black soul. Military life gave the black man control of his own piece of America. Military life gave him the keys to unlock the potential of his offspring. Military life gave him somewhat equal footing with his white counterpart. The confinement of the military gave black men their freedom. Leaving the military, the black man had education enough to navigate through white life and laws. The military gave World War II blacks things that other military blacks could only hope to see, but just a few got the chance to see what military service could offer in the way of freedom. The previous military veterans had to fight and die for an uncertain pension and uncertain freedom. The military broke some blacks, not through physical training but through mental anguish, by treating the enemy better than the black solider. With all the black soldier was willing to give, why was white so bent on holding him back, not allowing other whites to treat him as they saw fit? White had an unfair need to bar black progress as long as they could. What white did not know was black was his own worst enemy; all he needed was the freedom he craved; all white must do to hold black back had already been done; all that was left was to kill his spirit. As the 1960's commenced, here comes death.

Chapter 4

From Soldier to Convict

In America, black is more likely to be unemployed, underemployed, or jailed. In America, black evolved from free Africans, Africans without white clothing, without white formal education, or the need for any of those things. The African became educated, a thinker, and an inventor. So how did black go from soldier to convict?

While blacks in America were getting and given the opportunity to fight for whites and freedom, the great or infamous leader of the Zulu nation was being born, and vengeance would blind him with a single mission, war, along with death to his enemies and those he will claim as his enemies. From 1816 to his death in 1828, Shaka Zulu will drag southern Africa into and out of war, war the white way.

Shaka Zulu fought the way war had been fought by white for centuries. How is this important? From Shaka Zulu to General Colin Powell, black had the ability to fight. Only Shaka Zulu had won the respect of white people. Shaka would be the first black to develop war tactics that white will copy, at least the first to have it written down (Hannibal Barca was black-like). When the British found their way to the southern tip of Africa, they encountered a different type of African. The Zulu showed other Africans how war should and has been fought. The other parts of Africa - the parts that didn't get the fight gene that Shaka got – would be the parts that would supply America with free labor.

America never had the opportunity to see black skin at war, which could be why other countries had respect for black skin. Other countries fought black where it lived - where it could blend into the background.

Since the American Revolution, blacks have been in war, and war has been in black.

War was part of black, and not just the earthen battlefield, but the battlefield of his mind. Black was sent back to be enslaved after the Revolutionary War had stifled his hope, destroyed his dreams, and life had put him back in a box, but war would always be in black's box. This was a box white learned that they would always be able to open; black soldiers were a gift to whites keep on giving, with blacks willing to take only token appreciation in trade for their blood.

Black fought Native people, a people trying to get and keep their own land. White built up black pride: "All men are created equal." But black pride was built on the foundation of what white needed - freedom from the oppressor. Black fought with white to get Texas from the Mexican, and white built up black dreams.

Black men were given the pride of leadership that came with military command, the leadership of other black, as long as the top job went to white. With a little military bearing some blacks became men. Not all. But enough that black started to benefit from living in parts of America. Then black fought white to get his freedom and had his manhood built up, only to lose the one that delivered it: Abe Lincoln.

The black man roller coaster never stopped - only slowed down. After the war of northern aggression, southern whites felt the pull of black men standing upright; not since evolutionary times had black skin gotten such a gift. The ability to walk upright in the full view of whites was black men's award - a skewed award, an award long in coming, and an award with few perks to begin with. Greater perks would be fought for later, with time and more blood.

With the black man assisting in holding the country together, he was given his freedom. So, the definition of freedom had to change. Allowances had to be made.

The winners of the war of northern aggression had to tepidly protect the black man. If southern whites were allowed to have their way against the black man, then what can winning be called? Laws were written to protect the black man, only paper will not cut down a rope. Then the work and separation starts. From 1776 to 1865 war had seasoned the black man; his skin would not be his calling card for maltreatment, not always and not in all places. The fact that he could be and could have the same things as white - prosperity and problem - made the black man feel American black skin would be seen, but it will not be as black as the blacks that came before him.

The white man would now be his pain. The pain of the whip gives way to the pain of intolerance. Slave labor gives way to the cycle of indebtedness and the struggle of sharecropping.

After the Civil War, black saw the unpredictable nature of white. The same white that acknowledged that blacks were fighting for their freedom was just as quick to say there was nothing to be done when blacks were murdered.

1663: Beheadings - Gloucester County

1712: New York - 9 killed, 18 executed; Stono Rebellion 44 dead

1741: 31 Blacks dead

Before the American Revolution, black rebellion was met with severe punishment.

After the Civil War, Black Death was laced with fear and pain.

The Emancipation Proclamation was the reward for black participation in creating the ideal of a more perfect union - a perfect union for white control. Being black in post-Civil War America was little to no different than post-American Revolution. The same problem for black existed, with a holdover from slavery ever present: apathy. For post-war black, there were reasons to assume that with his sacrifices something would have to change, and something did, just not the way that black needed. Black needed more acceptance from white. Not respect. Not the respect black had earned through years of white warfare, just some semblance of acceptance. Just to be treated justly.

This would not be the case; freedom would be an anchor around the neck of black men, an anchor that drowned and hung him at the behest of any white that felt slighted in any way. Black veterans did not get the pension that was awarded to whites, and a wage gap developed, which established the beginning of a wealth gap between common white men and black men. While black was shedding his slave image and transforming into men and women, white was transforming as well. They were becoming teachers, and the lesson was that white leads, black follows. *Free* meant little to the multitude of free blacks. The lesson that white was about to teach would be more fearful than slavery and just as painful.

Slavery was organized; freedom was everyone for himself. Freedom came with responsibility to family (a somewhat new concept to some), home, for some, land. To white men, black freedom came with an identity crisis for them: Where would poor white, middle-class whites fit in? Without fanfare white had started a class system: at the bottom were poor whites, white could not compete in some of the more strenuous jobs, whereas if black died, so what? Get two more. If white died, there could be a problem, so to the bottom went poor whites. Black had status, and with it came the black class system, and with freedom, black begins an acknowledgement of their own class system. But where did he rank in the family of America? White men had to show black men that black freedom was not the same as white freedom, and they created a special group to spread the word.

KKK became the most feared three letters in America for black. White power served as education. For black it meant almost certain death, with a loss of property or a mass move in the middle of the night. This was the second blow in the loss of black pride and the opening of jail cells across America.

The end of the Civil War was the beginning of a reign of terror for the black man. Pulaski, Tennessee, soldiers hurting from the loss in battle, turned their skill to the one with the most to gain, black men. White men used the skill learned in war to terrorize black men and the family they were starting to build. White men allowed their loss and hatred to merge. The merger manifests in white sheets and horseback chaos. The Ku Klux Klan created in black man another defect, one that would allow most blacks to see white appearances - an appearance that will reinforce white superiority. After the arrival of the KKK the black man developed an unhealthy view of how white truly are; some will see white as a group to be feared, some black men will see white as glorious beings to be worshipped - not in a god-like manner, but in the manner as to be unable to achieve what white could achieve. Still other Black will hate and fear white. White's complete ownership of black start to crack with the brutality of the KKK. The black man's mind would not leave white ownership; only the body struggled for self-determination, while the mind would only bend away from white.

The Knights of the Ku Klux Klan bred in the black man a fear that no war could engender. Leaving the freedom of slavery meant finding out who could help you; as a slave, black men had value. A beating would get more work out of the slave, to keep the slave on the plantation. This was expected, but the KKK was different. The Black man was attacked for being successful, having too much money, harvesting better crops, or earning more education. Any perceived slight and the late night visit would bring untold terror - the hanging of the whole family, or just the father. The beating the wife would have to take while the husband watched. The fear in the eyes of black children burns straight into the brain to be recalled at future dates in stories and dreams, all to keep the black head bowed, back bent, and brain drained. The Klan not only bred fear into the black man's mind, but also corrupted the black image in America as well as everywhere else.

Being free after making a country wealthy meant giving something to the labor pool.

The Freedmen's Bureau was formed, providing black men their first knowledge of government assistance. While attempting to help the black man by peaceful means, the government made (in some cases) thing worse. The act of giving to black seemed to only pour fuel on a fire already raging out of control, white Southern pride. Forcing whites to treat the black man fairly will be a recurring theme in America.

The Birth of a Nation: Third Blow to Black Pride

When viewed by President Woodrow Wilson, it got two thumbs up! For the President of the United States to think that somehow black had taken over the South and no Southern white had to ask for assistance in keeping black underfoot stands as a testament to the power of cinema.

The D. W Griffith *Birth of a Nation* film did more for the Klan than the Klan did for themselves. D. W. Griffith did more against the black man than the Klan could have done. The capturing of white imagination, the view of the Klan as heroes fighting the good fight against the crazed black man, filled the void of losing a war. The rebranding of the black man from poor slave, to some, suggested that blacks would rape and kill - which was stronger than the whip and rope. This rebranding of blacks was to the black man more painful than any whip and just as deadly as the rope. The fact that white could imagine black in a superior position to white shows the conceited and arrogant bipolar nature of white as it relates to black. That whites would enslave, beat, rape, and skin blacks - and then be afraid of the victim – demonstrates the distorted image of the black-white relationship. To know the power of the black man's image is to control him and other whites. White power served as a form of currency.

White could control his slave image by controlling the script. The image of black could also control those whites that were sympathetic to the plight of blacks. *Birth of a Nation* also showed that whites knew how wrong slavery was by depicting the need for a white hero.

In the 1600's, blacks were just working slaves or indentured servants; they were learning a new language and a new people as well as a new place.

In the 1700's, black was assisting in the development a nation, learning a trade, and learning a religion - becoming a race. Black was learning what means white would go to and through for freedom. Although black learned these lessons, only a few could put this knowledge into practice. As with early white, black starts to leap forward. With every war and every President, Blacks gained more knowledge. Like early whites, one incarnation could not use the newfound knowledge or skill, so it was sent to the future body to use through genes. Separation, segregation, KKK, sharecropping: the black man of the 1800's was on the move. Upward mobility and his destination were separate but equal. He was in the North, business-minded. In the South, black was still farming, only now his own land.

After the death of President Lincoln, the black man's faith was shaken. If white hatred was so deep that the leaders of white could lose their lives for trying to be fair, what chance did the black man have?

Every chance.

The black man only had to keep his head down and let whites figure out how things were going to play out. And that what the black man did. When there was an occasion to fight, black fought, and when there were occasions to profit, the black man profited. When there were times to take advantage of others, black men did that, too!

After the Civil War, black men broke into three groups: the Northern black men, the Southern black men, and the free black men. Although all three groups were technically free, not all had the same idea of what that meant. The Northern black man fought to live and work where he chose. The southern black man fought to stay in his place and to own his own. The free black did all and neither; he went where white allowed him, and he had little to no opinion about local or world events. *Do not make waves* was to free black men words to live by or die by. Because the free black man so cherished his freedom that he allowed it to enslave him. The free black man neither had nor desired to have anything - no Northern education, no Southern work ethic; all free black men had was a sense of freedom and a fear of loss. The thought of losing what he perceived as freedom caused him to be enslaved to the whim of conflict and problems, big or small. With this came the need to ask for permission, ask for knowledge, and ask for acceptance. The free black man would become the nigger of today. Northern black man with centuries of fighting the good fight and centuries of semi-white acceptance started to grow beyond white control – the northern black began to shine.

He was aware of his station in America, he was aware of America's promise, he was aware of America's dream, and he has white support, somewhat.

The glow from Northern black shone a light on their progress, a light that immigrant whites needed to keep dim, at least until they could catch up. The Northern black man would also shine a light on Southern black, and this light became a beacon, which Southern black children would use to escape slave-minded whites and into the jaws of superior-minded whites. Northern black men became infected themselves, and some Southern blacks would receive the *pride* virus, and some received the *crime* gene. The Southern black man only wanted what he could work for: rights, land, and justice. The Southern black man was comfortable with his station in life.

The 1900's black man cannot contain all that he reads, all that he learns. With 300 years on American soil, centuries of black man's blood mixing in the soil, the Black man needs more from White. The influx of new whites to America stung the black man's soul. What black fought for years to get - new white gets in Day One? With every new white, black was pushed further and further back to the slave life - the life of work and invisibility. The 1900's introduces the black man to globe warfare.

In April 1917 the United States of America declared war on Germany. The First World War was at hand. While black had fought and died in wars before, this was a world war; it would be as close to early white battle as black man could get. This would be a battle on foreign soil, it was a chance to have white need black, but white had been in massive battle before. With black newfound freedom, taking him into a global battle was the last thing on the mind of white. Like the wars before, black participation was only a small stone removed from the wall of separate and unequal; black education would push, pull, and drag stone after stone away from the military wall until whites would get what they need - a ready supply of bodies begging to fight and die for white causes.

White needed military experience also, but not the fighting, just the paperwork - the paper that records their participation. The Black man needed all that came with a military obligation: education, bearing, and respect - not from white, although it would have been appreciated, but respect for himself. The Black man used the military to wash the stench of oppression off of him. No matter how hard the task, black would accomplish it; white could not hold down a man. A black solider in World War I could gain hero status fighting for the French or he could be given a meal for white soldiers. The Black man's knowledge of American promises of freedom and the reality of the deeds of Europeans complicated the black man's role in America. Why fight for freedom for others when blacks' freedom was fleeting at best and nonexistent at worst? To work, fight, and die for the French was a delight compared to fetching food and washing clothing for the black man's white countrymen. The knowledge gained in the war in Europe could not be contained. The compassion given by the French had to be shared. The treatment given by America had to change.

World War II started out like all wars before; black men would be given a service role, a small role in the fighting. White men would get the glory, and black men would get a postscript. The true inequality in every war that black fought in was not the demeaning treatment or inferior equipment; it was the lack of leadership training, the lack of military bearing that came with war. White men led soldiers in and out of battle. This not only served to make them heroes in the public eye, but also gave white men tools to develop business as well as keep and raise a family. This deletion for the black war experience would hamper black men's ability to succeed. As with most things American, not all blacks failed to achieve the full military experience; some excelled in all thing military. These men will learn from the white example how to conduct themselves. Their military bearing will guide them through and around the obstacles of life in America. Their bearing will also lead them away from other black men. The comic Chris Rock in his standup routine said, "There are black people and there are niggers; the niggers have got to go." So where did niggers come from - not the word, but the attitude? When black was introduce to America, he was a commodity. When black became a slave, he was treated as an animal. After the Civil War, black became a man, not yet whole, but being filled in to become complete. While in the mind of black his status never changes, the way in which he had to behave did change to some degree. The black man of today proudly boasts of being a descendent of an African king and queen; it is more likely that the black man of today is a descendent of a tribal leader and tribal member. Tribal black was more hunter-gatherer than an empire builder. Still, the transformation from hunter-gatherer to slave turned some blacks into niggers. The nigger gene comes from the effect of fear and death. After emancipation came the most fear-filled time in black man's American history. Free and educated black men were terror-filled, terrified of losing all they had gained. The thought of being killed paled in comparison to being enslaved again. These concerns pushed some blacks together. Post-Civil War black men knew what today's blacks do not, per the quote of Benjamin Franklin: "We must, indeed, all hang together or most assuredly we shall all hang separately." The birth of niggers started with black freedom, the gratitude to have it, the fear of losing it, and not knowing what to do with it. To be a nigger requires white participation – specifically, white apathy.

Apathy: lack of emotion, lack of interest or white attitude toward the plight of black men.

Where did white apathy come from? First, one must look to respect; who did white respect? Warriors, as white looked to war for many of its answers. White respect starts with war and battles won or lost, battles that show men willing to fight the good fight.

One example is the great African leader Shaka Zulu, the only African of early African history to present the British with a battle worth noting. Shaka Zulu is the key to unlocking white apathy toward black men. Dr. Martin Luther King, Jr., is the bridge that brings white apathy into the 21st century. When black is viewed from the pinnacle of a war machine, they are found to be lacking. Will blacks fight? Are they capable of learning? Will they defend?

Yes.

So why was it so easy to get so many to be slaves? In a country like the United States of America, why are so few black successful? These are questions asked by many other races. They cannot fathom an answer that could adequately answer this question. The answer is two-fold: war and black skin. Black has never waged war on a scale that could compare to other countries, with Shaka Zulu's battle being the closest to white war. Black has little to no experience in battle that involved thousands of soldiers fighting and killing with swords and shields: camaraderie formed in battle along with the courage to stand in all weather, and the willingness to fight and die for causes that may or may not be your cause. The ability to stand in the blood of a lifelong friend and not flinch. The ability to fight for hours or days to achieve the objective of a king or a general - people that often live better than you and your family. This is why white apathy flows from generation to generation. The lack of war experience hampers black progress and hardens white lack of empathy:

"My father came to this country with little to no money, and only the clothes on his back, and made a successful life for him and his family."

This type of thinking is used by other races with little variation. It is used to motivate family and to point to the failure of black. What is seldom mentioned is white skin, white countrymen, and the knowledge that comes from knowing the world of white. Immigrants came to this country knowing far more than the second and third generations of slaves. Immigrant came with the knowledge of food to feed their countryman, customs of their country, customs that could mirror the customs of America. Immigrants live in housing near others similar to them, with others helping to guide them to and through the New World. Success was, for most, a matter of taking. But not all immigrant were treated the same. Yet, the end result was always the same: *"Stay ahead of blacks by any means necessary."*

NINA: No Irish Need Apply

White discrimination against other whites was nothing new. With the advent of wealth, white started to separate themselves from each other. Ireland was the land where conquest or attempted conquest was met with brutal consequences. Here came the Irish to a land to be conquered.

When the Irish found their way to the New World, the welcome mat was well worn, but the Irish knew struggle and they knew war. That knowledge put them on a collision course with black. Black would fail. Not only would black fail, but they would make an enemy, and with the whole of America being white or white-like black, did not need another opponent. The weakness the Irish found in black skin gave them all the motivation they needed to succeed. Black weakness gave all who wanted a place at the white American table a common cause: Apathy.

The Irish discrimination was the first time whites gave a slim preference to blacks over another race of whites. This could have been a chance for black and a white race to carve out something together. But it did not happen. The Irish, like the future Mexicans, felt it was better to be discriminated against by American whites than to partner with an unproven man in battle. The fact that blacks would allow themselves to be slaves fostered white apathy.

The 1800's was the best and worst time for black men, with the dissolution of slavery and the rise of the KKK.

The 1900's were even better for black people.

The 20th century gave blacks the means to build their own obstacles. The mass migration to the north was seen by black as escaping any possible chance of their reintroduction into slavery or any of its off offshoots, such as sharecropping and forced incarceration. Young black people and the old that could travel left the South in droves. All wanted to be the first to succeed in the land of opportunity, or be the first from their family. The only problem was white was already there, and not just white, but all the white-like people. They were there and wanting, and the slave body was ripe for the picking. While black was free he lacked the skill to effectively navigate the North. Black already in the North welcomed the newly-freed black people. But they soon discovered that like white, black did not want the new black to outpace them. When new white immigrants came to America, white did not know how much to give and how much to hold back from the new arrivals. Northern blacks had some slave experience, but more freedom experience. Northern blacks also knew that America was there for the taking. They knew that the right place at the right time and a newly-free slave could outshine the old Northerner black.

Northern black wanted what was best for the Southern black, but not at his expense. In the South, black was finding his footing with the rise of the black family. The Southern black was becoming comfortable with his role with and without white people. Southern blacks were learning to use whites to their advantage. Blacks were working hard and gaining ground, opening small businesses, operating successful farms, and raising children. Then education changed everything. In the 1950's the so named greatest generation came out of the Second World War. The famous speech given by white President Franklin D. Roosevelt, "December 7, 1941 a date which will live in infamy," was for blacks.

Going to war was for everything. In war after war, black had sat by watching the United States preach righteousness to the world for its treatment of white-like people, all while allowing black to stew in a pot of inequality. This time white would not be allowed to only praise white soldiers; black would get his chance to stand on the parade ground and receive his accolades. While freeing yet another group of people that will surpass them on the scale of freedom and finance, blacks would finally be given a tepid show of respect, or at least the respect of soldiers, all soldiers black - and some white.

After the war, black was leaving the South and heading to the Promised Land, with echoes of black knowledge ringing in their ears: only be careful what you wish for, or deal with the devil you know. In the North, white could not hold black men down; in the North, black had years of freedom under his belt. Black men had years of fighting with white people for every inch that black thought he could get away with. In the North, black men had years of white help, with whites fighting for them. White could not hold the black man down in the North. He could, however, give the black man the means to hold himself down.

In 1860, Albert Niemann open the door for black man deconstruction when he chemically opened the coco plant. What World War II did for black-man pride and confidence, the Vietnam War took away. The Vietnam War saw America slip into the pantry of the past. The recipe for a successful war meant getting the right ingredient, with these first words: *"We hold these truths to be self-evident...."*

Second - anger: Boston tea party.

Third - blood: Boston massacre.

The Vietnam War had little of either. The Vietnam War was a throwback to European-style war, a war of what could happen, and Americans wanted little to do with war, especially one of a future they could not see, no. So if there was going to be a fight, send black. White was only interested in wars of glory and pride; black was still looking for himself, and the military was the father that held answers.

Vietnam was not the war blacks needed, Vietnam was the twisted step-father, the one that taught with pain and punishment.

"Is the stove hot?"

"I don't know; touch it and tell me."

Pain! Not paying attention in class dealing with land mines. Lose a leg. Punishment! Vietnam had hard lesson to teach, the two most important being white friendship and drugs. White friendship, blacks discovered, was like water: cold, hard, and for better or worse, ever present. White friendship could wash over you like a waterfall, or be difficult to find like a drought, but when you needed it, it was just beneath the surface. Drugs, on the other hand, was a *wow* moment for blacks. Drugs had been a part of white life for centuries. White had learned to disassemble their chemical properties, how to use them, and to a point, how to treat the addict. The 1960's centered on a hate war, so try drugs. White children needed a tribal ritual, something to push them into adulthood, just as war had pushed their parents. They chose peace - peace with war as a backdrop, and drugs for courage and inspiration. Black knew little of drugs. What they knew was white people were doing it, and that was good enough for them. Weed, acid, and pills were all the rage with white, and black assumed it would be okay for him. What black did not understand was white knowledge of treatment and white wealth, both of which black had a limited supply of. Heroin and cocaine provided the transportation and destination: transportation to incarceration, and destination to failure. The discovery of powder cocaine was a gun in the hand of a person that did not know how to use one. When white business owners needed to get more work out of dock worker, a little cocaine was a booster shot. This shot was not meant to sicken, but to prolong, to get as much work done as was inhumanly possible. A worker on cocaine was more productive, but after work he was a menace, not to white women as was written about in newspapers of the day, but a menace to his family and neighbors. In the late 1800's cocaine was used heavily by white, but only moderately by blacks. White would fight its battle with the addiction of all drugs, from opium to morphine to cocaine and beyond. But as with all battles whites fought, they learned and adapted quickly; drugs would be no different. Blacks, on the other hand, were the late-comers to the danger of drugs – again, a lack of education will cost the black family.

During the Civil War, medical care frequently meant amputation, but with amputation came infection and pain. Morphine took care of the pain and left its patience with the thirst for morphine. Soon whites would learn the cure was worse than the sickness.

Cocaine was next in a long line of half-measures in the search for a medical cure-all. While white was learning the lesson of medical mistakes, they were playing doctor on blacks. They gave black people drugs they knew to have side effects. Unknown drugs continued to be used for experimentation on blacks. In 1914, the Harrison Act gave black what could have been a way to avoid drugs, but ended up being fuel for the fire. With the government controlling drugs, blacks became dealers for whites. The harder a substance is to get, the more that people want it. The more that people want it, the harder it is not to sell it to them.

In 1960, California became the breeding ground for users of cocaine, marijuana, and other drugs. These were drugs that white knew how to control to a point, drugs whites knew how to get free of, drugs that were fun to share with newfound black friends. Black knew little about the drugs they were using, but if whites were using them, it was good enough for black, or so he thought.

In 1970, blacks were educating themselves, learning about the world and becoming a part of the melting pot of Americans. Drugs would be the chalk outline to the death of the black family. Vietnam vets returning from conflict in Southeast Asia would bring white thought back with them. The thought that white life was what black needed - the thought that black could have a white life, or that white would allow black to live as white. The 1960's allowed white children to see the discomfort visited on black by white, and for the most part the children of white did not want to follow in the footsteps of the parents. Some did; some white children would not be allowed to form opinions about black; rather, they would have it formed for them.

This separation of white was little different than white separation from the beginning of the republic. The only difference this time is black is on his feet, unsteadily, but standing. He has centuries of black blood, black American blood coursing through his body, but now black is learning that he has something that he did not get from his forefather. Black is learning that he has a white mind. It is not complete, so it fights with his black mind. This conflict gives black ideas that his life can mirror that of white. It can't. The white mind is not what white sees; white sees black skin, and white is not ready for black to stand on steady legs with a partial white mind. Black sees crime as an escape and sees drugs as an escape. Northern black cannot adjust to poverty; the family moved north to have a better life, but the only thing they found is a stagnant pond of poverty, government housing or ponds, ponds that held the poor. Black left homes in the south, left yards and nature to go North to brick and mortar ponds that held them in confinement - confinement from one another; confinement to one another. A program that was to be a hand up turns out to be concrete boots holding blacks down.

From 1865 to April 1968, blacks were patiently waiting for their turn at the American dream. After the assassination of Dr. Martin Luther King, black felt time had passed him by. Black felt that the time of playing by the rules was gone.

On November 22, 1963, the second president to openly hold out a hand to black people closed his eyes with bullets fired by white. For whatever reason black lost a friend.

On February 21, 1965, the second black to invade the mind of white lost his battle with black fear. Not since Nat Turner had white so feared the actions of a black man - Malcolm X. He was a powerful symbol of the manhood of the black man. While some black could not give in to white violence as was being taught in the South, Malcolm X was the pressure relief valve for black men.

On April 4, 1968, the flavor of what black people could become lay bleeding on the balcony of a now-infamous hotel. Martin Luther King, Jr., was one of a few to keep the country of black people from spiraling out of control. Dr. King was the soul of the unseeing, but much-felt soul of black men. With his death, black man's only solace was pride, and it was time to give that up. Robert F. Kennedy, who died on June 5, 1968, gave black men the right to expect government to protect and assist in the American dream. Kennedy taught black perseverance and to keep moving forward, only circumstance would not allow it. In the 1960's, black became upwardly mobile and politically active, making great strides.

Thus, the four men that held blacks together in a span of five years were gone. Black men were heading to jail in record numbers. All the ingredients were in place: No pride, the ability to persevere lacking, the manhood that held family together gone, and the mirror of respectability absent.

Crime. Drugs. Family abandonment. Welcome to prison, mental and physical.

Death was nothing new to black men; they had seen it and visited it on others, be it at war or at odds. The dying, along with the chance of hope, doomed blacks. In the beginning, black slaves seeing there were a glimmer of hope - good master or quick death - meant he could persevere a little longer; something was coming: peace or death. During the revelation the light brightened; still, it was only a glimmer, but now there were more choices: freedom was at the top, then freedom with property, or a good master, or quick death.

The Civil War brought even more choices. At the top was governmental rule of law for people of color, then property, family, work with pay and rules for payment, good boss, and long life. Long life was the start of blacks wanted to enjoy long and productive years; now black was starting to have things to live for instead of a cause to die for; the black light was shining brighter than ever before.

Bang! Lincoln is dead! The light is dimmed. Black will go out of the 1800's head bowed!

The beginning of the 1900's showed blacks all that white had done could be survived!

Black had taken the measure of whites and gotten up every time.

Dr. Martin Luther King gave voice to all the black men and women that had died before, and the ones that were willing to die then. Civil rights was the watch that ticked in the early to late 1960's. Dr. King bled and marched, marched and bled, for the right of black people. He used white media to show the arrogance and compassion of the United States to the world, which had put the United States at the head of the table. His use of non-violence would win the paper rights for black people, but not the civil rights of black people. On paper, blacks had the same rights as everyone else; in practice, white did as it chose. The death was not new; it was the glowing in the glimmer of hope.

By the late 1960's, black could not handle the dread of rain that poured down on them from every corner of the free and republic country, the nation that sent son and daughter off to war to free other people, all while enslaving, and entrapping the labor of the Black man.

Crime called to black men, and black men answered the call: Robbery in all its forms, purse snatching, breaking and entering, and even simple theft, nothing that was going to make black rich. Why? Because black lacked adequate education. Even trying to commit crime, black was inadequate. While black was robbing other blacks, the Italian, Irish, and other groups of white and white-like were getting rich. The first generation of poor immigrants knew more about life in America than third and fourth generations of black. They knew how to work the system; they knew that there was a system. Blacks only knew what they picked up on the fly, as to be a fly on the wall, as some black slaves learned, and at this time, television.

With all that black had to endure, with all eyes from other whites, with all that America had shown the world as to her intention, black needed to be pacified so white would stash them or at least some of them away in high-rise brick and mortar ponds. These ponds became stagnant to the point where you drowned, evaporated, or if it rained, welcomed it enough for the pond to overflow so you could escape. Not many escaped. These ponds started out as freshwater ponds; poverty made them stagnant. Poverty and inadequate education held blacks hostage in their pool of inequity. The lack of community soon broke down the former sons and daughters of slaves and sharecroppers who now practiced self-preservation.

Where there was once community support in the first wave of freed slaves, in the late 60's and 70,' *MINE* was the phrase of the time. Black learned to fear each other. Black learned to mistrust each other. Black absorbed the power and corruption of money. When black men started to buy and sell drugs, they abandoned home and family. Whether by jail, hell, or another reason, black men left their black families, leaving black women and black children to fend for themselves. The absence of black men wasn't new to the black woman. What was new was the lack of strength of the black woman. Black men with little knowledge of what it meant to be a father had little to no conscience when it came to leaving. As slaves, black men were laborers and sperm donors. When he was lucky enough to be given the opportunity, he could not be the man of the house. There were masters to contend with or white male relatives visiting the master, or anyone else looking for fun with the help. All children had to be taken care of by the black man. Children with blond hair and hazel eyes were the responsibility of the black man. The fact that his table was set for a child not of his making is further reason why black needed little reason to abandon his family. Looking at all white had and what little black man had pushed him to try and catch up, pushed him to be locked up, and pushed him to corrupt his gene pool. Black men in jail cascades black people downward.

The downward spiral of black man starts with freedom. With slavery there was separation, such as between house slave and field slave, but slaves told all that they were one people. Freedom showed blacks how to be master-like, how to use and abuse power and money. The have and the have not's were somewhat new to black, for some blacks to have more than other blacks from the same circumstance pitted black against other black. This also happened to other races. As with all things black and white, white was better prepared. White had safety personnel in place, and white had money to be taken and money to save. White had countrymen on the police force to protect them from non-countrymen. Black men had no such actions to implement, no saving, just other blacks to keep crime moving from black to black. While white could call the police to help, black could only invite another element into the flow of theft by taking. While certain white criminals held their neighborhood in high regard, most blacks were not as understanding. White criminals kept crime in balance; black had a free-for-all. While petty crime only entertained black criminals, the appearance of the drug trade fully engulfed them. The flame of drugs burned black to its core. As with white, drugs will be a scourge to the black race, only there will not be anyone to change the rules of the drug trade for black as the Congress did for white. The rules were in place, and the outcome was known. All that black had to do was avoid the pitfall that had befallen white years earlier. No such luck, black with his white mind wanted - wanted the cars, homes, money, and the monetary respect.

Respect. This was a critical value that he had seen white - the weakest white man – be given. The fact that he would use other blacks to get it was not a factor. The only factor was filling the need, the need to have. Heroin took a needle, so that could only infect the tip of the weakling and the ones that thought they were strong enough. Marijuana was smoking; it slowed you down, nothing that you should crave. Cocaine was a party drug mostly for the want-to-be-rich blacks. Crack was cheap; you could smoke and seldom would you die.

Black found his pot of gold. Two hours on the street, and you make more money than your father and mother. Two months, and you have more money than the people on your block. Fat, skinny, tall, short - if there were women, there was sex! Women wanted the money; women wanted the dope. Either way, sex was there for the taking.

Black had it all, with one problem. Other blacks wanted their pot of gold too, and now war would ring out on city streets, and all that did not go to jail went to cemeteries.

All of the casualties left the black woman alone.

Chapter 5

Failure of the Black Woman

Aboard a ship on the open ocean, FAILURE floats. Failure is coming to America. More precisely, it is coming to black America. It is wrapped it the guise of the black woman, but not the black woman of then, but the black woman to be. Failure is hidden in the inner depths of the long-ago black woman, the black woman that was pulled up onto a ship, filled with uncertainty and dread. The long-ago black woman would be infected with a time bomb - a bomb that would explode when she was at her weakest.

Failure means being confined in the black body of a female. It has been fertilized by her captor, a slave hunter. The long-ago black woman will give birth to the black woman of today, and the effect of her infection will steamroll across black America. The long-ago black woman's body and mind were shaped by events that the ship voyage set in motion. The slave ship caused the black woman to be cut off from the knowledge of her elders, not that their knowledge would have been adequate for the total life makeover that black woman would be forced to adopt. When African women were brought to America, they came with the knowledge that would be needed to grow - not only personal growth, but tribal growth, the growth of her people.

In early Africa her role was defined: support the tribe, run when the time warranted running, stand and fight when told. Cook, clean, marry well, and be productive.

In America her role was helter-skelter at best and brutally chaotic at its worst. Her African education would only sustain part of her and her future offspring. Mary McCloud Bethune said, "The true test of a race must be measured by the character of its womanhood" (AZ Quotes http://www.azquotes.com/quote/25986).

Despite this source of wisdom as a guide, black women are failing the black race of today! Why? Most will say that black men fail them.

Well, let's again start from the beginning. In the time of hunter-gathers, women decided which genes would stay and which would go. Women, not the clan, gave birth to a nation. In biblical times, Eve started man on the road out of Eden; she gave birth to Cain who went on to build a nation. Women since time immemorial have given birth, guidance, and knowledge to nation builders, without the assistance or with very little assistance from man, black or white. So how could black women failing be the product of the black man? She has from both biblical and evolutionary time not only held her own but has inspired wars to be fought in her honor, fought in wars, fought for rights that helped her cause - and held her back. All throughout history the woman has done well for herself and her race. So if the black man is not to blame for the shortcomings of today's black race, then what happened to the black woman? How could mother of us all go from being mother to bitch?

Knowledge.

This is the short answer. Today's black woman lacks knowledge; the knowledge that the long-ago black woman developed; the knowledge that grew with the rise of man; the knowledge that came from being enslaved. The post-Civil War black woman had such knowledge, but the knowledge that she had was lost and is needed to conquer the fast-paced change of the right-now.

What happened to the lead that the long-ago black woman gave her daughters? Like most things black, it goes back to the enslaved people. During the time of slavery it was the white man that initiated the decrease in knowledge of the black women. And like most things American, it happened in ways he could not have known: maybe. The first step in the loss of knowledge is sex. The raping of black women sent shock waves down below the surface of the black gene pool, creating waves that are still rippling today. The power of rape not only degrades the black woman but degrades her view of sex. The nature of sex to a pre-slave black woman was more for procreation than recreation. The pre-slave black was more concerned with the building of warriors and creating a strong bloodline than in having sex for enjoyment. Sex was to show the manhood of the man; sex was to keep the tribe strong.

What the pre-slave black woman had no way of knowing was the sexual habits of white, for white sex had long ago evolved into recreation. While black was learning his new role as a senior hunter gather, white had mastered the role as Homo sapiens, and with this mastery came free time. While no longer a hunter gatherer, white man had time - time that he used to create new sex names, methods, and performances. While blacks were learning their bodies, white were learning the bodies of everyone. Control of the entire body for sexual recreation would be the outcome.

White recreational sexual exploits would become pervasive and perverted, it would be one of the causes that the religious freedom seeker would use to leave for the New World. Sex became a tool for religion, mostly because of white men's abuse of white women. With sex the church was conflicted. Sex had its purpose, it was private for the most part, AND it was necessary and biblical. Sex was all things and nothing. Sex was money, power, and convenient; it could start wars or stop them. Whites' use of sex was as powerful as a weapon: sex in words AND SEX in pictures; sex was used to conquer and build strong alliances. White was establishing sexual position while black was depending on shamans and other worldly deities to have a healthy baby.

With a white healthy appetite for sex for sex sake, the unsuspecting, unknowing black woman experienced sex in ways that were as foreign as the land that trapped her.

White sex would scar generations of black families. The ripple that started in the barn and outhouse of the past gave rise to the uneducated teen mother of today.

Some think that black women failing is because there are too many babies having babies, but up until white decided that young girls would no longer be used by old men as property and sexual minion, girls married young. If a girl wasn't married by the time she was twenty, she was considered an old maid. A baby having babies has been around and is still around, and will continue to be around. The age of the person having the babies is not the problem; the problem is knowledge or a lack thereof.

The long-ago black woman learned that the age of the mother wasn't important; it was the support system that was key. The young mother had a support system, and that system knew how to comfort and educate the young, and more importantly, the young mother was willing to learn from her elders. Today that support system is missing, the knowledge is missing, and the willingness to listen and learn is missing. The embarrassment of rape long ago corrupted the education and understanding of sex for the black woman. She was unwilling to share her experience with the women that would have to experience it for themselves; she was unwilling to explain the color difference between her offspring; she was unwilling to live out loud the EXPERIENCE of sex in America. The silence of the long-ago black woman leaves a void in the knowledge of the future black woman, knowledge that is lacking and sorely needed then and now.

At one moment she is a worker or field hand, and then in an instant she is an animal, a breeder, and in nine months she will give birth to a life of black misery - misery and life events she could not control or not completely control. There were cases of infant death. A mother became willing to live the rest of her life knowing that she is a murder, a mother relishing the fact that she is a murderer. That is the power of rape; that is the power of the long-ago black woman. While adjusting to one role, the house slave, another role is piled on top of her young and unsure shoulders. Adjustment meant giving in to the absence of passion; how passionate can one be having sex with a man, just a man, some known, some unknown? And a black man that had little choice, a black man that could not protect, could not, not perform. A black man that with each act become a little less of the man he started as, a black man and ending up an animal - an animal that has failed to protect the pride, the herd, troop, or mob. While evolutionarily speaking he feels he is at the top of the food chain, being enslaved by white he learned the meaning of predator and prey.

With each act the woman retreats into herself; mindless, meaningless sex would harm not only early black woman, but give rise to race hatred, envy, and jealousy among black. Sex being what it was for the black woman had branches: sex with master, sex with black man; one that was chosen by her, and sex with one that was chosen for her. Sex with white that was chosen by her, and white that was chosen for her. Sex with master: being at the mercy or unmerciful power of anyone is traumatic, but to be locked into a take-it-or-take-your-life crisis is trauma untold. Having sex with the boss pales in comparison to having sex with someone that can take your life at any time for any reason. Living in the house of your tormentor and his children, along with his wife, presents indescribable mental anguish. Just the term "the lady of the house" would be offensive to any woman, especially one who would live with a man who nightly rapes the help. The "lady of the house" presides over a home that was more of a rape den to the black woman. What woman could or would allow another woman to knowingly have sex in her home or on family property?

White woman. Not only did white women semi-passively allow their men to have sex with the help, but also allowed them to have offspring. The resulting children in early life were allowed to play with half-brother and -sisters, but later in life would find that play time was over. The white man had no problem selling off the ill-gotten child. White men had more difficulty getting rid a dog or a horse than a mixed raced child. This forced abandonment would become a gene defect in the black woman - a defect of how much or how little ability to help the black male would be, could be, a defect that she would pass down to the black male.

Dating white (forced). Subsequent generations of free black women endured rape, some saw it for what it was, some fell for their tormentor. Everyone learned the power of white and sex. Some used what they had to get what they needed, and in turn corrupted themselves. Some relished the role of the live-in other woman, and some white women knew it. They saw that their husband was not theirs completely. The white woman knew she was sharing her white man with another. This acceptance of the relationship gave black women a way to get things and keep them; it also gave black women protection. Be nice to Mister Charlie and he will be good to you. While some black women were forced to date white, still others chose to keep themselves open to white. Their openness kept black men at bay, while being on call for whatever time white could give. This gave some black women status in their neighborhood. Everyone knows that she was with that honkey (someone that came to the edge of a black neighborhood and blew their horn). This was frowned upon in the community, but to the woman it was a necessary evil. To get where she thought she needed to be, she was required to use what she had. The free black woman had very little going for her but to become a cook, a housekeeper, stay on her feet to get to work, get on her knees at work, and be on her back at home.

The early black woman, the slave, did this. Her first generation of free black women did this, but as times changed, their hard work and sacrifices did not get transferred fully to the young black woman as with the black children to come. Early black women sent ill-informed black women to the future. As with sex education, the early black woman did not or could not fully educate her black daughter as to what her role could be or should be in the raising of the black nation. The early black woman was somewhat embarrassed to pass on the learning she had to do on her own, so instead of teaching the young black woman the perils of using what she had to get things, the young black woman used what she had to get what was wanted. Instead of teaching her daughter to listen and learn from white the elders, the black woman showed off her work ethic, which was only part of the education that young black woman needed. Teaching her black daughter how to cook, clean, and endure childbirth did little when it came to finding a husband and keeping him.

The post-slavery young black woman had other challenges to contend with. With white men making light skin a blessing and a curse, black women could not rave about their children's father; black women could not use their white fathers as a guide to show their daughters what to look for in a man. Sex being the taboo subject that white made it crippled the daughters of black women, who could not explain to their daughters how to enjoy sex or what to do in sexual situations. Sex would only be a small part of the missing education of black women; the early black women left a massive gap in the education of daughters, and the effect left large gaps in the education of the black man.

In the beginning the African man was turned into property like all other livestock. In the middle the free black man could only partially be a man, let alone a husband. In the beginning of the end the educated black man is a man in search of an identity.

When black woman was a slave, her maternal instinct was to be mother to all her children, her master's children and newly-bought young slaves. This was her life and mostly her choosing. That mothering instinct will have some future side effects. After the War between the States, black was free. The black woman was free. But: "FREEDOM IS A ROAD SELDOM TRAVELED BY THE MULTITUDE" stated Frederick Douglass (https://www.inspiringquotes.us/quotes/KHPX_Bhf7Ewky).

And there were a multitude of single black women, black women that viewed sex as somewhat dirty. When black was in Africa, clothes were optional the weather was mild, black had little or no notion that the body could not be pleasing to look at. Black did not see the need for embarrassment of the human form. Then white disrupted that view. Black women learned from white women, and white showed them that centuries of black tradition were not wrong but dirty only; white clothed black and made them think negatively about the human form. It should be covered; it should be kept pure because God was watching. The white showed black rape and that the black body could be used by men for sex to get things - and things were what a free woman needed. Her looks were for things; how a man looked was for things; did he look the part of a worker, did he look the part of a business man, or did he look as if he would always work for little or for someone? His skin color, face, size - all could be overlooked if he could provide home, food, and comfort. A free black woman was only a slave that could be educated. She still had the same problem as when she was a slave - she was a woman. But not just any woman - she was a black woman, only now she could decide whom she would bed with, to a point.

Only it was not much of a choice. She was choosing from men that stayed near the plantation. While some women made their way north, others stayed with what they knew. Dating black men: Two people that were ill suited to be together were free black men and free black women. In the beginning a black man could not be the man that a black woman needed. He could only prove to her that white was might. "In the middle of the night white men came to the house, drug my husband out of the house, tied him to a tree; I was in my night clothes one minute and naked the next. They made him watch as they took turns having their way with me." This could be said by almost any black woman, any place, with or without a tree. How can any man stay a man when he cannot even act the part of a man? He knows that she knows there wasn't anything he could have done. She knows that he knows there wasn't anything she could have done. They both know that their eyes will say things that can't be said. While enslaved, the black women learned (second-hand) that white would provide, provided that she knows how to keep her legs open and mouth closed. The problem with dating black men was the constant thought of "what?" What will he do for work? What will he do to help to raise kids? What to do if white comes? These problems plagued black life, but single black life meant fending for yourself against all odds. Marriage life meant all under the roof was to be taken care of, all. To be responsible for all meant catering to the whims of white. White boss had a bad day; its black had to watch out. Job slows down, black the first to go. White need a job, black had a job, black had to go.

No matter the suffering of black man, the black woman had it worst. Black had it bad at work. On whom did he take his white man's frustrations out on? The black woman. Lose his job, which was his pride manifested, the woman suffered. She did not suffer alone; either her children suffered with her or her friend suffered with her; her family suffered with her. The black man could hold his frustrations in or drink them in; mostly he suffered in silence. This suffering did little to help the black woman. The black woman needed the black man to protect and love her. The black man needed the black woman to love and help him. The problem was neither knew how to properly help. As a slave the black man was an animal partner to the black woman, used by white to breed with the black woman so she could bring forth other animals for work. In Africa the black man had his destiny in his hands; what he wanted to be was limited only by his ability. Finding a mate was just a matter of presenting himself as worthy.

In the New World, being worthy adopted a different meaning. Money - the ability to make it, keep it, and use it - was more important than any trinket or animal an African could come up with. In Africa the man was a man; some were manlier than others, but black could change his fortune by his will alone. How much was he willing to do? How far was he willing to go? It would not be the black that helped to fight the War Between the States that would benefit from the struggle of early black; it will be the offspring of the slave master.

During the 19th century black man and black woman were starting to get to know each other. More importantly they were getting to know the United States of America. They were getting to know their culture - their black culture as it related to being a black person in America. Black woman and black man were starting to grow together; they were starting to be a black family. Money, as with early white money, would bring forth the corruption of the black soul. While early white had its monetary influence in the 17th and 18th centuries, blacks were still dealing with being a senior hunter gatherer. While whites were killing and dying for wealth, blacks were still half-dressed.

In the dawn of the twentieth century, black would have to deal with his own monetary demon, and drugs lead the way for both black men and women. The black women of the 20th and 21st centuries blinded themselves to the power of money. They sold themselves as prostitutes without owning what they are doing. They paid men to be their sexual partners, all under the guise of being independent women.

Dating White: with race mixing, white gave black a color ticket, a ticket that could be and was used to escape black life. This ticket could be used to pass for white. With the uncertainty of black man's career opportunities, a black woman could be white. She could move away from prying eyes of family and friends and cross over to the right side of the tracks. To pass for white, the black woman had to betray the struggle of her forefathers and foremothers. Some blacks viewed this as the ultimate insult to the black race. This was a necessary evil; how could anyone begrudge someone trying to make a better life for themselves or their family?

It was easy. Black had the bad times etched onto their physical frame. Every black had a version of black skin. No matter the final hue, black knew the color of the black was slave-black - the black that first came over from Africa, and to give in to the purveyor of slave life was to say it was acceptable. To have light white skin and not use it to better yourself was equal to having money and not spending it. Light black had needs and a thirst, a thirst that black could not quench. Light black needed a white man, and so, too, did the black woman, not all, but a large number. They needed the knowledge that had been denied them. They needed the training that white had. The black woman needed to be made whole; she needed to have the courage and coldness that only white could provide. Some black women learned from the kitchen, some from the house, still other learned from the white woman. All women needed the education that came from white; the black woman needed it the most. Only the black woman could spread the knowledge effectively. The early black woman was a nurturing mother; she wanted what was best for all. While education could come from books, the education that black needed was from white people. Book learning was for children; black men and women needed to get help fast. The elderly black knew that their time was limited. They knew that telling their children to be like white folk was the best advice they could give.

"Be like white folk, but don't forget who you are."

With black woman, light white black woman dating white, the "don't forget who you are" message was rephrased:

"Forget who you were; concentrate on who you want to be."

Dating white gave light white black woman a different perspective on life. White taught to take what you want, and buy what you can't take. Money is money, family is family; don't mix the two. Light white black woman also learned that white was more accepting of those carrying themselves in a less-than-hostile manner. That mannerism made light white black woman more approachable to white, and the more approachable, the more likely that light white black woman could be accepted, or so they thought.

Light white black woman had two problems: white hate, and black impatience to the slow approach of liberty.

Light white black woman in their environment was included in all things white. The fact of skin color always lurks in the background. Just when light white black woman would forget, there were trips down South that would bring back all the feelings of black's first one hundred years, but for some it was a foregone conclusion that it would never happen.

Go back down to the pain and suffering?

No.

No matter, southerners could be found when one was least expected. Dating white meant black women could be somebody; the problem was being somebody to whom? Not black, and only in the presence of white could she be someone, but out of sight she was a conversation piece.

In 1619 the first of many slaves arrived in what will be America. When the Civil War ended in 1865, in 246 years, ten generations of black has endured slavery, rape, torture, threats, heat, and cold, and the entire process that comes with being trained to be an animal. So what if white power physically and mentally raped the body and mind of the black woman? What if white power emasculated the mind and body of the black male? What if white power corrupted the thinking of generations of young black children? What if white power enslaved the mind of Africans and African Americans alike? What if white power stopped the proper education of the black woman? What if white power kept her ancestors from being great teachers? What if white power raped her long-ago mother?

With the help of the black man, she and black as a whole should by now be able to pull themselves beyond the misdeeds of the past. So what's the problem? With blacks of today the answer is the evolution of the black woman: Her title, her education, her body, her transformation from mother of all, to African slave, to victim, and finally to bitch!

Chapter 6

From Mother to Bitch

What is the state of the black race and the black woman as they relate to the struggle of the white-black relationship?

The black race is lost and losing more every day.

Why?

Because the black woman doesn't know her place.

Where does she fit in? What is her role? Where does her education come from?

The black race is in a state of flux because the black woman does not know herself. She does not know her man. She has little understanding of what she should be.

Examples can be seen in the rise of same-sex relationships, the rise of women in prison, the rise of black women in adult entertainment, the rise in "leaked sex tapes", and the rise in sexual experimentation. Black women are forced into being single, and single parents, and parents of children that will never live with them or want to. From above the black woman is in conflict with the white woman for the more affluent black male. From below she is in conflict with the black woman of low moral standards. From the side she is in conflict with her understanding:

"I can do bad all by myself" and "I don't need no man."

While the single woman battle cry is correct, it does not tell the whole truth. As a drop the single black woman can do bad by herself; as a drop the single black woman does not need a man - but she is a drop. Whether she is a raindrop that makes thing grow or a teardrop that quenches pain. The drops make a pool, and the pool sends ripples forward and backward. The ripples can be good, or they can wipe away good. The drops coming from black women are washing away the good of the drops that came before her.

How does the caring, nurturing mother of all transform from mother to bitch?

Seeing the struggle of what was supposed to be a man, the black woman heart split in two halves. The halves saw the struggle of black men differently. One half saw the struggle as in need of help - help in the form of holding him up. The other half saw the black man struggle as needing a push. The two halves did not learn how to reconcile the strong approach with the soft approach, so this laceration was not repaired and caused the future black woman to be incomplete, and her halfhearted measure crippled the future black man. Black men in turn crippled black women.

From the 1850's to the 1950's were 100 years of looking and never finding - never finding a proper place to be. Blacks were tribal in their beginnings with tribal identity. There was no African, only this tribe or that one; no one name held meaning for all who dwelt in the land that white would call Africa. African would be the first identity crisis of black man. For white it was important to strip down the identity of his worker force. To allow them to be Zulu's or any other tribal name was to give comfort to live - in help, comfort that could be turned into a group and then into a gang - then into a fighting force to divide and conquer. For the first two hundred years white learned how to control black. Black had to learn how to band together; it would take two hundred years to come close. Black women were tribal from the beginning, only later losing their tribal strength with more education.

At the beginning of the 20th century after the end of the Civil War, the black-white alliance renamed black as "colored." Colored people became the fashion, so much so that they (black) organized themselves into the NAACP: National Association for the Advancement of Colored People. "Negros" is a name to which well-meaning white use to give some quality to black life, and like most well-meaning white, their help will hurt more: *Negro* will grow into *nigger*. The term that can steam open some black like a clam, *nigger* is a term that could have come from white without proper education, which leads to improper pronunciation. No matter how it came to be, white made it their word, and *black* and *nigger* forged a root that ties black to their slave past.

Black identity crisis lingered on even after black stopped allowing white to name them and started to name themselves. So the African / Negro / nigger became simply black, but there were now more black intellectuals, and they were of different hues of black and brown. The more education black received, the more they ached for an identity they could claim as their own.

In the beginning of and into 1900's the black world was changing and black in the middle of a cyclone. Upward mobility black was fighting the good fight, no longer asking but demanding and organizing. The cyclone will twist and pull black in every direction. Black mind will grow, black children will grow and America will grow both black and white America. But danger comes with growth, growth that is built in a cyclone will break apart or stay together forever. White was standing by to pick up the pieces of the black kingdom - a kingdom that white was allowing black to build, hoping and thinking that black would fail and oblige them or give in to their temptation. It would take some major sacrifices to achieve black downfall, but white was used to scarifying a king for a pawn.

The 1940's, 50's, and 60's were decades of freedom, and black women were on the move. They became singers, movie stars, workers, and constantly mothers. Black men were keeping up step for step educationally, but emotionally, not so much. The twentieth century gave black a new lease on life in America.

Black people became upwardly mobile. The black family was becoming a unit for the first time in black history. Black men's skill and patriotism in battle was starting to be acknowledged. The military discipline that white had received was now being felt by black. The ownership of his children was being felt by the black man; the willingness to fight the good fight, win or lose, was strengthening the back of the black race.

Then the 1960's began, with the fracturing of the black psyche, the black woman, and the black family version of the trail of tears or the black man version of the Bataan death march. The decade of the 1960s was a stumbling block for black and death led the way. While black men were mourning the loss of great black men, women were moving on. As mothers they could not fully mourn what had been lost. With the death of bodies came a sickness that black hadn't experienced since his freedom:

Who am I?

"Say it loud - I'm black and I'm proud." The godfather of soul James Brown took to the stage to give a shot at trying to ease the identity crisis of black, and did so, for a large part of the black population. Being proud to be black put black on a get-money course, and education led the way for some, but the sickness did not go away; it simply lay dormant, waiting for black to stumble - and black men would stumble. While Martin Luther King was preaching non-violence, others were preaching violence, and still others were practicing violence. They were educated in the outward appearance of America, not fully aware of the inside workings of America. They thought that if America was not going to turn the other cheek, they would no longer turn the other cheek. This level of teaching and thinking would be the undoing of years of marching and beatings suffered at the hand of white by the civil right leaders and black victims as a whole. The violence teaching of some in the 1960's was misguided at its base and misinformed at its height. The misinformed started to think in terms of getting back at white; they began to commit crimes with the misguided notion that they must and would be treated as white criminals. The 1960's also introduced black to drugs; more destructively, it introduced the black woman to drugs. While the 1960's were mostly about white kids' rebellion against the success of their parents, drugs were a part of the rebellion. But there was also a save-the-earth vibe to the 60's, so the drug of choice became marijuana - a cheap drug that could be smoked.

Misinformation and misguidance sent large numbers of black men to jail in the 60's and 70's, which meant the black woman would revert to the prevailing perspective following the Civil War. Yet the 1960's Black woman's life was seen to be better than the life of her slave mother.

Drugs were part of the party scene. While some black women used drugs, most still had their mother's warning fresh in their head: don't trust, know your surroundings, and know your friend.

Work, lack of black fathers, drugs, and jail - the black woman is for the first time on her own. After the Civil War there was a tribal effort to keep everyone together. During the first and second world wars there was an all-for-one effort, with a little bigotry sprinkled around. During the civil rights struggle came an effort to keep everyone moving forward. In the 1970's the black mood changed; there were no longer an effort to be as tribal as before. Why? Lack of men and an increase in the activities men could choose from. Black freedom was collapsing in on them. The volume of work the black woman had to choose from meant too much freedom. Work meant she could take care of herself to a point, because work meant she could not be in two places at the same time. She was a full-time worker, but a part-time mother. Ms. Part-time mother will cause a gap in the love and discipline of her children. Ms. Full-time worker will cause a gap in the role of men. A woman that doesn't need a man makes a weak man weaker. A woman that doesn't need a man makes a strong man weary and leery. Without the traditional role, black men fail the black family. Black men fail to understand how to help or how to fit in; without traditional roles, black men are lost.

During the death decade of the 1960's, black men mourn and rebel, all without the black woman. During the drug craze / crime spree of the 1970's the black woman was left to fend for herself, and she did so all the way up to the 1980's.

The black woman is looking for a helpmate, not a helper. A black woman sees the change she wants to make; what she doesn't see is she is outpacing the black man and in effect outpacing her future and putting her children's future in doubt. What she couldn't see was the effect that drugs will have on her. The working black woman with children put the children in chaos. They see other mothers with their children; at home, they see the effect of mother working. What they don't see is the reasoning. Why? Why can't they have the home mother and working father? The working mother doesn't educate her children well enough to understand why she has to work, and wants to work. The black woman fails to show her children how working makes the black race strong. She is not aware of the damage she is inflicting on her children.

Welfare is a program from the government - a social program that will further baffle the black woman's children. Why work? Why leave home when you can get a free check like other mothers? The black woman work ethic was not fully explained to her children. The fact that she works should have showed how hard work would pay the bills, how hard work meant you were free to do what your money allowed you to do. The black woman work ethic only showed her children that hard work meant you were always tired; you had little time for your children and even less time for yourself. The black woman was in a no-win situation. Why? Because of where she lived, and what her neighbors were doing (one bad apple spoils the bunch). It is difficult to tell your children that hard work is better than getting a free check and free food.

It was not only black woman, but in the cases where there was a black man, their hard work did the opposite of what they were intended to do. Welfare meant free money, free food, and more time for kids. Only not all mothers used their free time to raise kids; some used their free time to entertain themselves and men, not to educate their kids or make sure the kids educated themselves. Hard work was a no-win situation for both black men and women. One bad apple spoils the bunch; in the north with its close living quarters (one to another) each family problem was shared with everyone, whether by accident or design.

In the South, a family lived in houses with yards with distance between, but in the North families live closer together. This causes family to know a lot about each other. Welfare for one meant all knew. The free flow of money stifled black children. In the beginning, northern black looked at welfare as a handout, as something to be ashamed of, but as with all things black, the sickness of *who am I?* It caused pride to slowly fade away.

In the North, welfare was seen as giving up on having pride. Welfare was seen as not having the willingness to try, but *who am I?* It broke down black's resistance. The freedom that blacks so vigorously fought for was now drowning them. With so much to have, black could not organize his thoughts into what to do first. So he did what he knew, and not all had the same knowledge. Take what the white man owes you. Take what the white gives you. Use what the white man gives you and make more. The taker soon found out that like black freedom, free was not free. Free money or what appeared to be free money was paid for with corruption - corruption few black would escape, but more importantly, the corruption would ripple through their offspring, effects that are felt today, the poor willing to stay in that state.

What about the educated black family? The one that showed their children that you could work hard and not wear yourself out? These were the ones that took what white gave them and used that to make more. These blacks would be the blacks that black would use to attack black education and make it not the cool thing to have.

The educated black took what white gave and added to it: free money, land, free education, work, work, money, and all the reasoning to move away from poor black - poor black and the bus. In 1954 desegregation of schools started the descent of black education. Black education was difficult enough when dealing with other poor black kids, but to not be smart in the company of white kids tore black kids apart from each other. Uneducated black kids prompted the black woman's slide from mother to all, to woman, then to bitch.

Chapter 7

The Children are Our Future?

The educated black family gave black something and someone to look up to, but the educated black only wanted the poor black to look and not touch. That is, look to them as inspiration, but do not live close to them, and do not come between them and white.

White wanted to keep distance from the educated black as well as the poor black. Only the educated black kept fighting to move where white moved, to go where white went. Neither group wanted anything to do with poor black. As a child, watching grown-ups pull away from you burns; it was a hardening of the black child heart – a heart that was diamond pure was burned into cheap coal, coal that would make young black, black inside and out.

As a poor black parent, this separation was seen on a battlefield, and on this battlefield poor black had to be tough, so a hardening of the black heart was the answer. Right? As black parent has done in every era, they taught their children to be tough. This was their slave thinking, their Jim Crow-era thinking. The hardening of the black child would serve as a platform - a platform to fall from. Educated black knew things poor black had to learn; white knew things both had to learn. Poor black being so far behind the start of forced integration only gave them the incentive to quit. Educated black could "act white": use proper pronunciation of words, speak in a softer tone, mask their exterior with words and deeds that mirror the words and deeds white felt were appropriate. Poor black could not be "acting white", and living in a world of predator means to fight your way everywhere. "Acting white" in the poor black mind was equated with being docile, never mind all the act of violence white had perpetrated all over the world.

"Acting white" did not mean you could not show off your intelligence or that you could not be intelligent; it meant not showing up others. You could be superior, but not act superior. "Acting white" by speaking in a soft tone was an invitation to fight; not accepting an invitation to fight meant you were weak. Weakness equals prey, and prey could only prey.

Why?

Poor black parent - slave-minded black parent.

"Stop crying!"

"I'll give you something to cry about!"

"If someone hit you, hit them back!"

"Stop telling all the time!"

These are classic poor black parents' teaching tools. This is what helped get black through slavery, the latter half of the 1800's, and into the 1900's. Poor black parents did not notice that their teaching style was causing black children to bring forth the thing they were trying to avoid - turning their children into the needy. A poor black tough exterior made getting an education nearly impossible. Poor black parents failed to give their children a way out, a safe house when they did not succeed.

There should have been a place for them to retreat to; when white children failed, white blamed the school, the system, and ultimately themselves. Then they blamed their children's health, white got medicine, hired tutors, and did whatever it took to get their children the best education they could buy. When poor black could not take school anymore, they had idle time and a tough exterior. Poor black had been indoctrinated into believing *tough* means never giving in or giving up. *Never* was too much time, too much time to hold off teasing, too much time having your failure pointed out, too much time watching your life fall further and further behind. *Never*, without a release button, is too much time - time to commit crime, time to think about getting left behind; time to watch friends learn and grow, and move closer to the black-educated family. The poor black child had time to think about letting down the black family. Poor black needed a way to hold back as many blacks as he could. "Acting white" became the battle cry: going to school, trying to be like the white man. Off to college to be the white man's nigger; thoughts of success; begging the white man for a job. Anything that stopped blacks from leaving poor black, poor black used it, and used it to great effect - so much so that it is still uses today by street gangs.

In the beginning of the 1970's, blacks were holding each other back with drugs, prostitution, and other criminal enterprises. Black were using black children and the black woman. To black folks this was not as bad as it seemed; some black children and parents saw it as a teachable moment because in the 70's, black were also covering the backs of the hopeful; even drug dealers and other crime figures looked out for the few that showed promise. Others saw this as a lifestyle, something to emulate. It wasn't until the 1980's that black failure in education and parenting would be truly seen.

Crack: crack head, crack babies. These terms will come to describe black failure. With wealth, black came to know idle hands.

As white kings, farmers, and land-owners in Europe learned after the hard work had been lessened, the effect of idle hands would cause a scourge to appear, be it war for war's sake or sex because of boredom. Idleness often causes a population's downfall. Crack hit the street like a virus, a virus dispensing money, sex, and sorrow. The educated as well as the uneducated will bear witness to the stifling of a race. The black population watched in horror the carnage of black-on-black crime, a brutality that white had somewhat weaned themselves off decades earlier, with the failed attempt to stop the sale of liquor. Black of the 1980's had not known the lynch mob mentality of pre- and post-Civil War white. They did not understand the destructiveness of the fear they inflicted on the consciousness of fellow blacks. The bloodshed white had spilled from black, young black, was now visited on each other. The amount of bloodshed in the name of money would rival bloodshed in the name of the king, which was only second to bloodshed in the name of religion.

Crack was unlike other drugs; it was king, it was religion, and it was prayed to, worshipped, and feared. For black, in the beginning it was seen as a passive drug; it was smoked, unlike heroin, which was injected into the body, crack was like smoking weed. Smoking weed was something black had learned from white, something that black had been taught by well-meaning young white as not being bad for you. Weed was part of being educated without the books, a subtle side effect of drug education by the uneducated. Weed was just a plant; white learned that other cultures smoked it without side effects. Educated black with white friends taught it to other black, and with the white seal of approval, weed was okay. Cocaine was for the well-to-do, but with a little chemistry, cocaine would be brought to the common man.

With the lack of education, the common man and woman will sell their all to keep the high coming. The black man will sell his freedom to get high, and divorce himself from life to get high.

None of this comes close to what the black woman sells. The black woman sells the black future, in the form of children: crack babies. Black children lose the black father, brother, and most importantly, black pride, pride that kept even the black criminal respectful of the black woman. With the crime wave, young black lost himself in a world he was not prepared for, a world without supervision, with mother working or smoking, friends either in school, in jail, or on the street, the young black had no future. Men were now rivals; women were bitches - sexual playthings. Mothers were few; fathers were nearly non-existent. With her two halves of a heart the black woman saw a man as someone to take care of more than ever before. Without a valid argument to have mother abandon her children to the street, the child chose street life over home, so what argument was there to have.

"You live under my roof - you follow my rules."

Crack was not only a drug addiction for the user, but the seller as well. Crack did not kill, but turn black into the walking dead. There came hours of walking to find who was getting high and how to get in with them, hours of walking to find money to get high, hours of depression after getting high, and getting high to alleviate the depression from getting high.

Black women had little disposable income. What they had was their bodies, and for the first time young black men and boys had no fear of black women. Young boys hustling for young men had money. Young black women caught up in drug usage needed money, and early in the drug trade, sex was currency. Young boys seduced by pretty women gave the women the upper hand, but only for a short time. Young black boys having sex with women the age of their mothers lost more than their virginity; they lost respect for their sexual conquest, they lost respect for sex, and more importantly, they lost respect for women in general - and the black women most of all.

Black women tried to convince themselves that it was only sex. In their mind it was only sex, but in the black community; the black woman held the black soul, the very essence of being black. Every alleyway that felt the bent knee of the black woman was left with a piece of the black soul. In the ripping open of the crack wrapper was a ripping away of the black soul. Every baby born addicted to crack was a future postponement or never to be. Every stroke the young black male took shortened the future of himself and his peers.

"Just sex" was and is a misunderstanding of the female body; sex holds the key to pride for every race, and with black playing a game already in progress, pride was the most important piece the black race had.

Crack did more than introduce young black males to war. It introduced young black to poetry.

Rap - with a hip hop. Rapper delight opens up a world that would open up a race. Rap and drugs went together like a slave and a whip, and as with the slave and the whip, some rebel, others quickly surrender, and still others use what they had to get what they wanted. But as with slavery, the biggest winner is and has always been white. Rapping was the cotton of the 80's, and drugs were used to whip the blacks into submission. Rap was entertaining in the beginning, but soon turned dark, the outcome of idle hands. Rap pointed out imperfections in the black community: law enforcement, black men and black women, and the effects of drug and alcohol.

The pain of the young black male can be heard in rap music. The pride that was lost can be seen in every rap video. The thought of his pain can be seen in every scantily-dressed black woman. The hollowness of the black future can be viewed in every black face. The black man had become a prisoner to his mind and his circumstance, and a physical prisoner. The black woman has become a shadow of her former self, a shape with little to no depth. The fading of the black race was at hand.

Every year black moved further and faster away from being black folk, black folk the fourth generation of black, the first to be considered people. The first to take what white had given and make it uniquely theirs. Black folks were the ones that had sit-down Sunday dinners, the Black folk that held their family secrets, the Black folk put their trust in their pastor and their faith in their Lord, the Black folk that put education in the hand of teacher and a belt on the behind of the child, Black folk that would rather lose a child to the street because of parental decisions, and not the child's. Black folks that wanted what white people had but with no need to be where white people were. Black folk that did not have a need to live around white people or eat around white people. Black folk that knew what black pride was, and how to show it. Black folk that wanted to be called into white society out of need or want, not barge into somewhere they were not wanted. Black folk that knew how to be Black and American, and not have white tell them who or what was cool, what was in or what was to be done.

Black folks are different from black people. Black people are a race of humans named by white people, and Black folks are black people with tradition, common sense, morals. The traditions (at least most of them) of Africa were lost or beaten out of existence by white, so black in America had to install their own. And they did; they taught young black how to navigate the white world, how to avoid the crime world, and the cost of not knowing. With the struggle of Black folks, black became not just a false classification of brown-skinned people, it became an identity to wear an identity to identify with, but that level of pride will be short-lived.

With drug wealth and other crimes, these traditions have fallen into the blackness of the slave era, along with dark skin, and most Black folks of the 1960's and 70's knew their identity.

With rap and drugs making black nigger-rich, black identity and skin color starts to fade. Being nigger-rich means no more food that reminded black of the poor South. Nigger-rich black must eat food that white deems appropriate. Southern vegetables are replaced with Asian cuisine. A car cannot just be a car; it has to be a rolling apartment, with paint to direct the police to someone who is in need of harassing. The Afro of the 70's with its pride-filled style gives way to the moisture-filled jheri curl with it mixed-up identity, black skin, white-like hair. The 60's soul sista and the 70's brick house were replaced with "a bitch ain't nothing but a bitch."

The 80's rap music shone a spotlight on the plight of black people as it related to governmental help, or lack thereof.

The 90's rap music made black problem glow, as rap started telling of black decline. Rappers told of police brutality, inadequate housing, an inferior education system, all valid points, but then rappers start to shine a light on the black family - absent father, neglectful mother, unruly son, and unashamed sister.

Are the children our future?

Not for many black families. The young have little to nothing to identify with. As white morphs into incarnation after incarnation, so, too, did American black, just not so evolutionary. Black only moved from name to name, from African to black to colored, to Negro. Black's constantly shifting identity at least gave them something to be, something to do. Blacks had to build themselves an identity. Young blacks have no past - at least no past to hold on to, so their future is bleak. The past for young black is clouded. Lack of Sunday dinner with grandmother and grandfather means history is lost. Lost history means their past is no different than a movie. Their future is written at the governmental budget office: how much to spend on prison, welfare etc… How did young black get so far off the path their ancestor had set them on so many years earlier?

Freedom. The Black man and Black woman were freed without education, or without a proper education. A large number of young black males have never been given a bath by a man, an activity that doctors think may create a bond between parent and child; the warm water and touch could mean something to the child, a mimicking of life in the womb. The mid-1980's in some families was a time when young black children had to fend for themselves, forcing them to grow past their childhood. A large number of young males have never been hugged by a man, at best a nice chest bump, but still no male affection. Today, the thought of a man showing affection to a child brings up the deepest fear of all parents, a fear that plagues step-parent lives.

Gang life. All races of Americans have had to unite and form groups to help them fight other groups. But as with all things black, even gang life was ill thought-out. Without black tradition, without a tribal identity, without strong role models, without the continued presence of a male, young blacks fill the void with destruction. Without positive affection, young black looks for affection - and gang life offers affection. This is where young black receives male affection; this is where young black gets the tribal life his mind tells he should be receiving.

Rap music. An unforeseen side effect was gang life, barbarians, which like the white variety of barbarians of the past, black gangs become the scourge from the likes of Attila. Only unlike Attila, the young black gang had no idea what they were doing. Attila had a need that morphed into a want. Young black had a want that went nowhere; young black did not know how to need - they were not taught how to struggle; they were only taught how to get around the struggle. No matter the amount of money young black had, he would not leave his surroundings. Black fear held him in a prison of his parents' making. Attila fought for the good of his people, and the greed of what he saw white had. Young black fought his people. Attila put fear into the mind of his enemies. Young black put fear into the mind of his own people. Gangs became the tribal life that young blacks needed, only there was no leadership. There was a leader, but inferior education meant no guidance. Tribal life instills what is needed to move from child to young adult, and then to adulthood, something that is missing in all black community and especially the young black male. All of blacks' time in America there was a leader and communal living, tribal living. Tribal life meant structure; family life was limited in what it could offer. A tribe had a leader, and there were others against whom young blacks could measure themselves. There were rituals that young black could perform. There were ways to measure his flow into adulthood.

Government housing was a stifling pond of reflection; the only way to prove anything to anyone was to fight. And fighting meant war, and war meant an escalation in armament. Hand-to-hand moved to sticks, sticks to knives, knives to guns, and guns to stupidity, stupidity to a homosexual lifestyle or down low. The lack of positive male and female role models leads young black to confuse affection with sex. Young black males trapped by money and gang life enter prison much earlier than the young body and mind can handle. Early incarceration means lack of females, but the mind still tells the body that the sexual peak is coming, even if females are not. Testosterone tells the body that it has energy that needs to be released. The result: youthful rape.

At first it is difficult to comprehend male on male, but as quickly as it starts, it's over. First it's shameful, then it's evolutionary - survival of the fittest. Then the shame-filled turn on the weakest. After years, it is only something to do; it's just sex!

After years in youth detention and a few years in prison, young black is a man. His life is now on the straight and narrow, or so it seems. Black marries, but it's not complete; sex is not fulfilling young black years of boy on boy and man on man. Specific types of sex have been imprinted on his mind; he has spent his prime sexual time in the company of other males. His mind can only imprint his first-time one time; from then on, young black has only one first love, because he has equated sex with affection and power. He has not had an affectionate male in his life, at least not one that did not want something from him. He is confused and at a loss as to what to do. Who to talk to? How to start a conversation that you don't want to have? Who will care? Will you be viewed as weak? What if someone finds out without hearing your side? Questions swirl as the mind crumbles freedom, a dead weight around the neck of the freed. The only comfort is the confinement that spawned the thought demons.

Young black female took a longer time to get to the homosexual lifestyle, partly because she was told to take care of the black male. As time passed, young black female starts to see other young black female carrying the babies of young black male - the young black males that were at the parties while the young black female was locked in at home. The young black female starts to tire of "love said, but sex meant." Sex without any sort of commitment sends the young black female to do for herself.

Mother who is ill-educated, working, trying to get her groove on and find a man for herself left young black female to wonder: how does it feel to be loved? Young boy wanted sex and to play; older men wanted a show pony. What about a woman; what could she be to the young black female? All - she could be all that the uniform young black woman wanted, and she could be everything that the young black male wasn't, in theory, of course. The black woman had equal affection for her son and black daughter; she simply in some cases did not know how to show it. Hugs and well wishes were replaced with things like shoes, clothes, makeup, and perfume, things that only made her grow up faster. The hard life that black lived was passed down to the kids, and it stole all the softer side that life had to offer. Black women without a black man shortened the life quality of young black females. A young black female without a male role model has little to no idea how the male mind works. She does not get to see how dads treat moms, only how moms treat the men that mom hopes will be her man. She has no one to bounce ideas off about boys, so she has to learn by trial and error. Only the error that she may and oftentimes does make is a life lesson, and a drain on black life.

To say that babies having babies is equated with the blind leading the blind is misleading. The *who* of having the child is only important to the cry of a stable family dealing with the unstable situation. Age is less of a problem than education. Black grandmother fondling a grandchild is afraid to ask the new mother, "Who's the father?" The grandmother is seemingly going to be there to assist in caring for her grandchild, then the young black female discovers grandmother is lonely and in need of male company, so babysitting is out. The false hope is worse than the age of the mother. The age of the mother is less of a problem than an "I-bought-this" father. The father only buys things for a child that is destined to fall through the cracks of life. The age can be made negligible if affection is tempered with logic, and parenting, but this does not often happen. The new baby smell is replaced by homework sweat and needs. Attention fades away like the new baby smell. Then the young black female is alone.

The young black male from the beginning of his youthful American life has been the river that carries black life into the next generation. As a slave, he was more valuable than his white peer. He was the fire to warm the soul of the black woman. The two together struggled through a boat ride of confinement and death; the two struggled through learning the rule of slavery. The two struggled through the trials of being free. The two struggled through whipping, war, and love lost. The two made it through all just to watch as white took the lives of President Kennedy, Malcolm X, Dr. Martin Luther King Jr., and Robert Kennedy. Malcolm X on the surface was not killed by white; it was black corruption by white that took the life of Malcolm X. It was the succession of death that caused the black man and black woman to venture away from the path they were set on by early black.

The black woman thoughts of what an American family needs: "A good man, a man to love me for me."

What the black man thought the American family needs: "I'm looking for a good black woman, a woman like my mother. I just hope that my kids are healthy."

The thoughts and words of the misguided black man and woman - what is a good woman? Someone to follow, someone to share, someone to lead?

What does the black woman mean by "a good man"? More often than not they are unsure. Looking at the divorce rate, both have one thing in mind - only to end up with feeling, "I felt he/she was the one."

The black man wants a woman like his mother, but only to a point. Where the point ends is as varied as black men. If the mother was not a good mother, then he is lost and will almost always have to choose over and over again to try to find what he saw good in his mother. After the drug craze of the 1980's and 90's, the value of the black woman went down. The mass abundance of sex and money held and had by certain young black men brought about an indifference toward the black woman. Nearly any man with a couple of dollars could have a Romanesque-style orgy. The more money to spend, the more black men devalued the black woman. While many black women avoided the drug wave, it did little to increase their stock. The availability of cheap sex drew some of the best black men into the fray.

The younger age that a black starts to have sex, the harder it is to educate him and her as to what he and she should be looking for in a mate. The younger a black starts to have sex, the earlier he starts to devalue black women. Rap videos and stripper poles: black women saw the money that rappers and drug dealers were making, they also saw the money that orgy girls were making, and they saw what white had seen years before. Lease your body - men will pay for the convenience of sex, sex without strings, and the kinkier the better. Women were willing to lease their bodies, not to the man, but to the money.

If selling their body was too harsh, they did the next best/worst thing: show it off. Half-dressed, undressed, bumping and grinding, whatever the money called for. For some black women, children would be what the money called for, and their number would increase with every successful rapper or neighborhood drug kingpin. The black woman not caught up in the groundswell of female degradation became a victim of it as if by osmosis. If a black woman carried herself in the manner that befits a woman, she was viewed as being above the common black; the "acting white" of being black is having and being prideful. Why? Because black coming out of the 70's lost the identity black folks had built. The black identity of the late 60's and all of the 70's was this: We are all moving up, and we will all help each other. The education system was beginning to hire black teachers, blacks were learning with white, meaning they had better tools. Dr. King's death only showed young black that white only respected might. Malcolm X's death showed young black that there was little black could do that white could not take away. So when the white radicals bid a farewell to 1969, blacks took what young white had showed them into the 70's, when black started to have an all-for-one attitude, and a get-educated attitude. Even prison life was enriched, and with that came money.

The wealth and idleness of black was as dangerous as it had been for early Rome, all the power without the education to handle it. Black women that tried to save themselves for marriage found out how futile it was when their man was found to frequent crack addict, prostitutes, and any manner of woman that was looking for "a good man" or quick money. A large number of black women were lost to what a good man was, and most are still today. The early black woman passed on to her younger self what she knew at the time to be true. Cook, clean, and please your man, give him strong children and raise his children, and keep a little money for yourself, just in case. Do what you have to do to keep your man. Do what you must to take a man; don't live your life alone.

In the beginning this was the best advice early black woman could give. What happened was the next generation failed to adapt this knowledge to the times. With the black woman working and the black man going to jail, the black woman took the advice of the early black woman and put it to use with her son, making him the head of the household, without allowing him to earn it. The black woman tried to make for herself a non-sexual husband. With all the pain and suffering the black woman witnessed the black man going though, she put hope in the only man she could only partially control. The black woman needed a man that would be there for her.

With disappointment after disappointment in the black man that was to be hers and hers alone, she turned to her son. The early black woman needed and wanted her son to be strong, wanted him to go out into the world and make something of himself. So if he came back, early black woman could point with pride at what she had accomplished; she had made the black race stronger.

So, what changed? The early black woman had a built-in advantage - black men with no desire to leave the plantation life meant a steady "husband". The few that knew the advantage of living in the North went: some to educate themselves, others for work they could be proud to perform. The black man that wanted stability knew that he must make his stand where he was. The early black woman overlooked the early black man's indiscretion; she did what was good for the family. Why? She was locked into her position. She was the body of the house. All she really knew was what she had and what she could learn from white and people coming by. She did not have the education that black woman would one day gain.

The black woman of the 70's and 80's had a built-in disadvantage - an incomplete education. Incomplete meant in the form of formal education, and incomplete in the form of mother-daughter education. The early black woman's education was what she learned; her later self-education was what she found out. The early black woman learned through trial and error, and passed it all on to the daughter. The trial and the error of later black woman was she found out things that she failed to trust in, and in most cases failed to pass on. The later black would push her children on a merry-go-round of failure. The later black woman was caught in an education loop - she had too much and needed more. The education she received from early black woman needed to be adapted to her current state. She couldn't properly adapt all she knew with all she was learning, and the loop continues.

The drug craze pitted black son against black men, because often, the father was gone and mother needed a substitute, the not-quite stepfather. If the man was strong, he and the stepson at least got along, but if he was weak, conflict arose. In any conflict some concessions have to be made, and most importantly the warring parties need someone to referee and some allies. The black woman had choices to make: defend the son against the man, or defend the man against the son - all bad choices, or they appeared that way to the black woman. She did not have the education to reason out her options; she did not have the education that she needed.

The education she needed was in the head of the white woman. White women had years to struggle through these types of conflict; some learned, but some didn't - from the Egyptian women making their sons pharaohs, to Roman women making sons emperors and senators. White women learned and taught each other the power of putting men in power, white women had dealt with decisions that black women were just learning about. The choice was not the man or the son; the choice was what was best for the woman, and this was what she did not know. What could the son become? What could the man provide? What was in her best interests? She did not know because she did not fully understand herself. She had little encouragement from her mother, a mother that oftentimes was in conflict as to how much success she wanted her daughter to have.

As a mother, some felt they given up too much to be mothers and wives, and why should the daughter's life be better than hers? What if she had to move away from her mother? She doesn't get the built-in babysitter, the child doesn't get the grandmother, and so elder education is lost. What if she was under unmanageable stress, what if she was pushed into being a parent, or what if her dreams were put on hold to care for the daughter she wasn't sure she wanted? With all of her motherly sacrifices, the daughter can be all she could be, but not the mother.

Before she became a mother, her environment did little to force her to leave, but everything to make her stay. Make her complacent - make her comfortable in her mired state. She could only decide her fate based on a fairy tale, a lie: love.

The black woman had and has had love; the emotion confused with love the word for *fairy tale*. Having a man say the word and perform the act that they both call love is totally different than the outcome from love, the emotion. The first part of the lie is the white lie, fairy tales black had heard read to them from early black life in (free) America to early black childhood here and now. Books and movies claimed the word *love* was key to life everlasting. Black woman had only a partial understanding of the black man she was for the most part stuck with. Her understanding was sex, food, and a clean house, and he should stay with her forever because he had said the magic word – *love*.

The second part of the lie – sex.

"If you really love me…,"

"Don't worry; I will love you even if something happens."

Lies.

For decades the black woman followed the code with little variation, even reading her younger self the same fairy tale that was read to her, and furthering the lie of *love*, the word. The now-black women have a somewhat stronger grasp on the knowledge of self, but love remains elusive. Some are chasing the fairytale; others are chasing the want. ("I want a good man") The problem now is the absence of fatherly advice and motherly affection. When black stayed close to family, there was always relief. If the children needed to be fed, they just went to grandmother's house. Father needs to vent, so he went to the shop, barber or mechanic. He listened to older men talk, took what he needed, and left the rest.

With wealth, black moved to the fast life; small town living could not contain their newfound knowledge and money. Leaving the small town meant there had to be something to show for leaving - things. There had to be things to show why you left your father and mother on their own. So, black got money and bought things. They bought themselves out of being black folk. They wanted to live where white lived. They wanted to live like white, and eat and play just like the white people. Only they did not ask their children what *they* wanted.

The children of today are adjusting to the white-like life. Unlike the children of forced busing, today's black children don't face the same blatant hatred, just the worst kind of racism, quite the kind that you don't see coming, the wink and the gun kind, where white winks his eye and pretends to shoot with his hand, a way of saying *good job, good boy, good girl*. You are doing a good job; now show white how it's done. Then white has your job, a job that now pays more money, because white needs more money for his family than black needed for his.

The future of the black child is indeed a very mixed bag; where will they take their black children? Where will they take the black race? The new black child will enter an America that has seen war go from brutal hand-to-hand combat to the death, to laser-guided missile and live-feed of war. The new black child will learn this new form of war as kids before them learned: at play in the form of video games - all the death and destruction in the convenience of their room - a room that is bigger than the home of their ancestors. The world that the new black child will enter will be softer than the one black skin entered eons ago. This softer world will be for the new black child an opportunity, an opportunity for the first time in recorded history of black skin that the new black child will truly be able to achieve things that were only possible for early black at the cost of his soul. The task of achieving these great things will only be hampered by the one thing that has been the curse of black life - to answer to the haunting question, *who am I?*

For the new black child this question rings louder, but somewhat hollow. The thing that America has to offer the future American is fewer than the things that early black had at their fingertips. Early black had a strong will, a strong body and a country to help build, and when the country got up and running, free black had centuries of knowledge to learn in years, and wars to fight. Educated black had centuries to learn how to handle prosperity, and the less educated black had centuries of back-breaking work to contend with.

The new black child will have to learn how to handle pain, how to grieve, how to properly grieve, and how to handle adversity. The new black child must answer the question, *who am I?* Only this time the question will be more difficult, and the answer more fluid. The new black child is a mishmash of racial identity. The early black child was also a mixture, but for the most part a hidden/unhidden mixture, while the father was only known by the mother; options were not many. The new black child is a sometimes-planned, sometimes-unplanned event; with races living closer together, intermingling was unavoidable. The new black child is black and white at his or her base, but the outer core is everything but black or white; only the mind is still colored. Free black tried to breed this mixture out of his offspring; he wanted to be racially free. Other free black tried to breed more white into his offspring, as he needed them to be racially acceptable. Still other free black had to learn who he was, or what he was, and what he was to become. Educated black wanted to overlook his skin and focus on his mind, focus on his ability, to allow wealth to define him and his family. Other educated black wanted white to define him, and white saw past the skin to the money, but only so far ahead. The great death of the 1960's put on the back burner the black quest to answer the question of, *who am I?*

Black had to deal with drugs and violence. The new black child will not only have to define his blackness, but also his Americanisms. The new black child is a product of America's melting pot ideal. But his immigrant part will always need defending; his blackness will always be in question. What it means to be black has always been different. To early black, it meant to gain acceptance; to free black, it meant to compete. To educated black, it meant melting into the American dream, to future black it is going to mean finding an identity. Black now use terms such as *biracial* as if now is the only time he has had the blood of others running through his veins. The biracial term is his feeble attempt to gain ground on his identity by not physically dealing with it. Black moved from livestock to property, and to black folk, but then the thought disappeared. He wanted to disappear, but with his blackness intact. He could not have it both ways, so he shunned what he thought was his blackness. He slicked his and her hair, changed his and her diet, spoke softer and more cautiously; black changed everything he could and then he moved away from the thing that reminded him of himself and herself. He took the even more drastic step of attempting to marry away from himself and herself. Black did all he could to walk away from his and her blackness. The only thing he could not do was to get white to go along with his changes. White only saw dressed-up black skin.

The new black child will have the first opportunity to be seen as a person, but it will only be an opportunity, because he will bear the burden of caring the dead weight of the incarcerated. The educated of today is leaving a massive amount of dead weight to be dragged into the future, the should-have-been-educated.

Millions of children of black and mixed race are waiting to be rescued by the new black child. The new black child will, for the first time in black history, deal with millions of men and women that have little to no pride, little to no direction, and little to no drive. Black has always had the ability to stand on his own two feet, be it work or crime. Black did what he had to do to struggle on, and today, black can seldom make sweat mean anything meaningful.

The new black child will be saddled with what to do with ageing parents and convicted aunts and uncles getting out of confinement. The new black child will be responsible for less money and more burdens than any black generation before. Their reaction will be different than the generation before.

Why?

Compassion. In the generation before, black folk took pride in caring for the elders of the family. The closeness of the black family was to note the sacrifices made to maintain the family. Now black openly defies both the parent and the grandparent. Their lack of firm and soft role model forces them to harden themselves outside while becoming brittle within. Tattoos, piercing, starvation diets, and suicide were the direct property of white. With today's black identity crisis in full swing, his mental health is now in decline. The black of today are only descendants of the black that fought for the right to fight. Today's black are not the strong black that endured the crossing of an ocean. Today's black most often never learned to swim. Today's black are only descendants of the black that had little, but managed to raise many on what there was. Today's black are only descendants of the parent that raised both white and their own kids. Today's black are only descendants of the black parent that comics made famous for their discipline.

Today's black are only descendants of the black folk that walk for a year to achieve what only death could achieve for the multitude of black: rights. Are the children our future? Yes, but they are only black future selves; black is his own future, and his future is fading. He has giving up on trying to defend himself, given up on trying to be viewed as an equal to white. Black has proven that only time heals all wounds, but nothing heals the scars. The wound of slavery has been healed over by the deeds of white for black, although the mind of black is filled with views of slavery and techniques of slavery. Black has allowed the pain to subside. Slaves' pain once lead black to march and change, but today's black marching is all for show. The marches that lead to beating and death are now the march to vogue in front of cameras. The march that held white at bay is now used by white to point to the absurd nature of the black people of today. The black that plowed the land that would one day become

America is now the light brown skin of the vegan. The Sunday dinner that was used to repair black pride is now used to show who has what, or who has had the latest medical or technical treatment. Church that was used to build a community is now a place of worship. Faith that heals the black nation is stymied by money and fame. The fading of black started with white injection of DNA, but it shifted to black being uncomfortable in white sight, in their black skin. Then it shifted again to black being preferred by white because of the shade of black skin.

The final shift came when the white woman became comfortable with skin other than white. The mixing of black skin is not the fading that black is dying from; it is the fading of the black way of life - the food, family, and faith guidance that once were the hallmarks of what it meant to be black. This is the true fading of black life in America, and blacks will one day find that they both miss what being black was and loathe the faded copy of what being a *nigga* is today. What role did white have in the fading of black life, and what role is white continuing to have?

Television.

Chapter 8:

Black / White Apathy

From the first flicker of the camera, white would hold black financial, political, and social life on film. With *The Birth of a Nation*, D. W. Griffin told America a story. He revealed to America that life as they knew it was or could be over. D. W. Griffin had discovered that a picture was worth a thousand words. He showed that the entertainment industry could make change in the minds of millions. With the advent of motion picture, a story could be shown and told. The ability to make people fall in love with a character could be used to make people hate a character as well, and mistrust a race. The motion picture could be used for good as well as not-so-good. The outcome of a story was left up to the men with the capital.

In the beginning, with few exceptions, movies were meant to entertain, and make money doing it. With black, there was little to no money for paid entertainment, so movie moguls made movies for the people that could and would spend money. White people: there were movies about white people to entertain white people. Occasionally there were black people in early movie to entertain white people. But the early black faces were oftentimes white people with black faces. The true black faces were never seen in a favorable light - or at least not favorable to black eyes.

Why?

The quick answer was racism.

The longer answer is money and lack of knowledge. The early moguls were immigrants. Their knowledge of black was most often told to them or viewed from a distance. Often, knowledge of black was not needed; black was only there to get a laugh, do menial jobs, save whites, or make white look heroic, all the while making immigrant white wealthy. Early movies were not used to uplift people; they were used to uplift a nation. Early movies gave movie goers the America of the Constitution, the America that people are told that exists, the picture postcard America.

While movie makers were making picturesque America, they were also hampering the growth of black. While some of their movies were meant to entertain, there were also subliminal messages sent out into the movie-going world. Malicious? Maybe or maybe not;

at this date no one can be sure - only the mogul knows for sure. What is absolute is the feeling people had and continue to have about black; these feelings are directly related to what they see in movies. Foreign whites also have feeling about American whites that are closely related to what they see in movies. It is this reasoning that designates America as the destination for all seeking the American dream, or the American dream of the movie. This is not to say that the movie version of America is fiction; to the contrary: "There is gold in them thar hills." The only problem is a pecking order, as to who gets to look for said gold, and the top of the food chain is white power.

As the movie industry grew, so, too, did white wealth and the black-white divide. Only a few blacks could get invited into the gold that was movie-making, and black saw and felt the absence of dark skin. The absence of dark skin was preferable to some blacks; they would rather not see any black on the screen than to see another stereotypical black. The great Hattie McDaniel is reported to have said, "I would rather play a maid than to be one." This was and is the sentiment of many blacks chasing the Hollywood dream.

What effect does this thinking have on the psyche of black? One thing it tells black is to get the money; it will buy you respect (it won't). The second is to get the money and forget the respect (impossible). Third, it tells black that white makes right (true-ish). When viewed from the perspective of the receiver - roles such as maid, butler, and nincompoops, there does not seem to be anything wrong with making the money. But when viewed as a black nation, it flows though the mind of every would-be employer, loan officer, judge, and police officer. When simple-minded views from movies find their way on to the black public, then white cannot be held responsible for treating black in an unfair manner, i.e., police shootings. While the early mogul may have started the stereotyping accidentally, what about now? The same difference. Black are more likely to be put in roles that should be beneath them, but are not.

The money: Why would black read scripts that show they will not be taken serious or knowing they are going to die quickly? Understanding that they will be humiliated, why would anyone intentionally sign up to be treated in such a way? The answer to the question is two questions.

Who am I?

-and-

Where do I belong?

These are the two main reasons that black is willing to be mistreated. These are the questions that give whites their power. These questions force other races, especially black, to ask and to try to answer. For other races, the whiter the skin, the easier the answer.

"We are white-like."

Change the accent and modify the name - and there you are. The darker the skin, the easier it is for the question to send the questioner down a darker hole. When it comes to black, there is no good answer.

Am I American?

Am I African?

Am I African American?

If I am American, then why do I not fit in?

If I am African, why don't I understand or care about Africa?

If I am African American, why is it black that I feel?

Am I black?

While whites did not intentionally present these questions to anyone, they simply stepped aside and allowed other races to fight for their affection. Other races fought and continue to fight to see who will get to be second to American white. As with the American wars, black sought to get skin in the game. The movie era was also about black trying to get skin in the game. Black could not lose his place in the America to come, so he was willing to show white that no matter the obstacle, he and his were more than willing to be at white's side.

The 1960s offered a glimpse into white life. White was, for the first time, ashamed of his children, and the children their parents. White felt that his children could upset the balance of power. Free love, mixed race sex - no longer were white women taboo to black men. Absent of racial hate in white children made light of racial hatred to glow brightly on old white ideas. White was reminiscing of the early Civil War and could not - and would not - go through that again, neither for white children nor black people.

The 1970s was the first time in black history that blacks were truly free. This decade saw a decrease in hostility; whites of the 1960s were growing up and taking stock of their lives, and so, too, were blacks. The death decade showed blacks that the time for getting was **now**, and the black woman led the way, complete with television roles to match. Blacks had been invited into the television world, or at least the black woman was invited; movies were most often segregation lite. She came with some stereotyping, just not overtly. She was slave-maid sassy, slave-maid heavy, and had a slave owner touch for discipline. Black men in movies and on television were still typecast, but the type was getting better. Black men were even typecasting themselves in the movies they made, for example, pimps with white women wanting them. Everything that white had showed them would sell, blacks now did. Only in the 70s, black embraced it, mostly.

As television advanced, so did black apathy and white control on what blacks thought. Television showed white taking care of black as only white could or would do. Television showed black taking care of white as only black could or would do. Television in the 70s also showed other races that black and white had a special relationship; this could be accidental, but it started a wave through other races of color to compete with black for white approval.

In the 1960s, the closest thing to white acceptance was Jewish acceptance of black. While their acceptance was mostly conditional, it was more than other whites were willing to give. The condition that Jews put on blacks was "struggle, and we will struggle with you." Accepting the Jewish hand meant respecting their conflict that came from being different in a place that sometimes punished people that were different. Black had heard the true feeling of American white toward their Jewish neighbor, and blacks could not control their feelings about Jews. While black respected what the Jewish community was willing to endure on their behalf, it only complicated the black mind. In order for black to accept the Jewish hand, it meant pushing away the hand of American white - somewhat. It meant to put Jews between American white and themselves. That could not be done, being akin to leaving mother for a friend.

Jews started the film industry, moved to television, and is responsible for black character or caricature. Their hardship was mirrored by the hardship faced by black. They did not have the clout to fight slavery in the early years, but during the battle for black rights, they could not stand on the sidelines again. But once again black could not accept the help of just any white; it had to be the right white - the white that white approved of, the white that held black at bay at every turn. The white that makes black loath to be black. After the death decade of the 60s, the best of the 70s and the drug craze of the 80s and 90s, black lost what it meant to be African and gained more of what it meant to be an American, and that was what black is today - an American. In the America that has been homogenized, black has had his Africanisms milked out of him; he is more American than black, more American than man, and that was perfectly okay with him. Time and money did what slave owner could not do to his ancestors: neutered him and replaced his passion with apathy!

How? Was it some Tuskegee-like experiment? Was it some great conspiracy? No, it was what everyone that has been in a relationship knows. Make them want you, play hard to get, and they will try harder. Pay them little to no attention, and they will crave you. Whether white did these things intentionally or not, the result was and is the same. Black craves white things. Some crave the people themselves; some crave the people to the point of erasing their blackness. The passionless black in his quest to fondle whiteness gives up his black passion. His ancestors fight to be free is replaced by suburbia. His ancestors' fight for civil rights is replaced by membership in mega-churches. His ancestors' fight for the right to fight is replaced by black-on-black crime and stop snitching slogans. The freedom rider of the 60s is replaced by rappers.

Black apathy built up steadily and slowly, so slowly that black was aware that he was becoming complacent. He was not aware that the military that he fought so hard to be a part of was now actively courting him. He was not aware that the white soldier that he had wanted to fight beside was slowly leaving the military for better jobs. He did not know that the military that shunned him and his kind for decades now was giving him the death that he wanted. Black was fighting for right that he was receiving, but in some cases, was unable to handle, such as fighting for the right to go to school with white children, not understanding the pain and pressure that would be associated with this request, nor understanding the hatred that white could have. Black did not truly understand the toll that all the fighting would have.

Apathy. From the time black was brought to America his fight started - the fight to build the original colonies, along with challenges like weather, natives, bugs, language, and customs. Fights that formed a country, fighting through a century of being less than a man, slightly more than an animal. Fights through night terror and lynching. Fights for the right to fight. Fights for the right to be included.

Black at this point is fighting for the right to be the shadow of the entire race of great fighters that came before him. He has little in the tank to fight for anything more than to trade on the legacy of the true African American. Black in America is now only a title. What it means to be a black man was assassinated in the death decade of the 1960s with Malcolm X's educated passion. Dr. Martin Luther King educated blacks about patience. What it means to be a black woman was slowly smoked, sexed, and degraded away in the drug-induce 80s and 90s; now men are tattooed brats, and women are their willing playthings. Mothers are friends; dads are visitors. All are in search of the almighty dollar, that which separates *you* from *you all*.

Today's black is more willing to commit a crime than stand up for another black or stand up to white for a black face. Today's black is more willing to go to jail than school. Today's black is more willing to fight than vote. Black-on-black crime is overlooked and almost expected, white on-black crime is a pot boiling over, especially if it is government-related. Police top the list. Police-related crime on black has a long and colorful history, which gives black all the reasoning in the world to push back when it comes to police and crime. Today, all across America, black men are being released from prison thanks to DNA. These men were at the mercy of police corruption, and after years of spending their life's capital locked away, now they get their freedom.

Apathy forces young men and now women to accept that their life is not worth fighting for. The lawyer that you paid for will talk on your behalf, but will only work within the limits put on him by the judge or prosecutor. He will seldom if ever work through those limits.

Why?

He is more often than not attending social functions with the people that make the rules. He cannot and will not upset the apple cart. He will play his part, a part that only money will change. Having black people you know go to jail for reasons that can't be identified in a court of law plays with the psyche of the black mind, a mind that is filled with southern stories of lynching, killing, and torture. A mind filled with fighting and losing after the war is won. Black apathy in these circumstances is understandable, but cannot be accepted, just understood. The pain and struggle of early black was greater than anything today's black can imagine. The pain of early black was married with mind torture in a union that spawns today's movies. Nothing that today's black endures can come close. Still, black apathy excels in the black mind, unwilling to lead in black struggle, unwilling to help the black unfortunate, unwilling to see black skin as a fight from across the ocean.

My vote won't count.

These white people will do what they want.

You are wasting your time marching.

These are the voices of all the excuses, little of the money.

"You are not acting black enough."

Translation: "The stereotype that we came up with sounds more aggressive, talks more uneducated - we want the black person we created."

In early movies the black character was singing, dancing, or taking care of household duties. These characters knew what was asked of them; they knew what it paid. The work was good, and the pay better; it was a status symbol job. No matter the degrading nature, blacks were on the big screen, and few blacks could say the same. Some whites could not say the same. To be an actor was more than a career - it was allowing people to dream through you. Could anything be better?

For black, things could always be better and worse. The black actor was willing to take the worst of the best they could get.

What of today's black actor? What are they willing to take - pretty much the same? In most cases the racist feeling of the bygone era is waning, not gone, but waning.

Why? Why is it that with all of America's accomplishments there is still pocket of racist feeling? There are famous people married to opposite race people. There are white grandmothers that have never had a black person in their house, that are now raising their biracial grandchildren. In the past few drug-filled decades, the number of biracial children has spiked, and with that realization so, too, have the number of non-drug induced mixed race relationships. The number of mixed raced children rivals the number that came about through sexual conquests in slavery. With all of the mixing of races, racism still is prevalent in the land of the free, home of the brave.

Why?

It could be that what passes for racism today is only white apathy. With the swearing-in of the first biracial president, racism was openly heard; white apathy was only a part of white-black life together. During the twenty-first century in the most diverse country on the globe, ape comments from the nineteenth and twentieth centuries are uttered. The racist picture, a picture that would be at home in any movie or television show, depicts the black-white struggle in America and on television, only now it is on the news, showing how far white and black have come in their race relations. In all honesty, the black-white relationship has only grown larger, while staying the same.

In times of slavery, some black had it better than others, thanks to someone white, as it is today. During the Great Depression, some black fared better than some white, as it is today. During World War II, black fighter pilots were requested by white, some. Just as some white requests a ball player today. The number of whites that don't like blacks is percentage-wise nearly the same; the number that are willing to deal with black for the green, percentage-wise is nearly the same. Only dating and marriage has changed. Black and white relationships are not stared at as long as they once were. Relationships that were once a death sentence are now commonplace.

Why?

Movies and television.

The continuation of racist behavior and mixed race relationships being accepted can all be traced to television and movies. Sammy Davis, Jr. was not only a part of the Rat Pack, he was accepted as a part of white life. Sidney Poitier was given an opportunity of a black lifetime to star in a film - and not just any film - but a film that was to entertain; not entertain in a manner of a fool, but to use his talents, not just his skin. To be an actor, not a punchline, and he did not disappoint. *No Way Out* sent him on his way to being liked - to be liked by black and white alike. Sammy Davis, Sidney Poitier, Nat King Cole, and a few others were a drug-induced high to some blacks, a high that they wanted to experience again and again. They wanted the white life, the life they saw these few blacks enjoy.

Again, white gives black just enough to keep them coming back for more. Black actors as with black music brought white to a point where they were accepting black, just not getting too close. The more that white tries to stay away, the more their children move closer. The more the children move closer, the easier it is to overlook the black-white divide.

While the Klan isn't burning crosses in the yard of a mixed race couple, racism still thrives, and now movies and television are as much a hindrance as they help. While some high profile actor and actresses are seemingly given a white pass, others are given menial roles. These are not the same menial roles of the past; these roles are viewed on the surface as just part of the movie or television-making process. Sidney Poitier's greatest movie showed him to be the man that white wanted all black to strive to become: educated, strong, and without flaw, a willing helpmate with ideas, and a willing spirit. Strong and docile - someone that white would not be afraid to approach.

The black man that white feared most and still fears is the one that they create in movies and television: The thief, rapist, thug, the hard-to-kill black, the one that only wants white death and white women.

The horror movies; where the running joke is that the black person is the first to die or is the comic relief. Although his fears are not the stuff of make-believe; it is easily traced back to his beginning, but just not as meekly as the movie suggests. The movies simply brings to the screen something that everyone knows and accepts, everyone meaning white and white-like. The problem comes when black is not given the opportunity to be somewhat heroic, when his fear is played up to the point where he or she is barely more than a punchline then the man or woman can't be taken seriously or taken too serious(cops). Is there no room for playing up this fear? Always, but there should be times where black is also more heroic.

The subliminal message that plagues black in movies and television is not just a local thing; it is broadcast to the world.

TV Show: A pretty special agent is approached by two men - one black and one white, both bigger than she. A fight ensues; she quickly dispatches the black guy and turns to the white guy. While everyone knows she is the star and is going to win, her fight with the white guy is a fight. The black guy never had a chance; even in the world of television, a black guy can be made to look as if he can fight.

TV Show: An anthropologist walks through an airport, and behind her is a large black man; she feels threatened and quickly tosses him to the ground and begins to question him, only to find out that he is airport security. He was given a job in security, but he can't protect himself from a female scientist - not that it could not happen, just why black?

For the guy it was better than not working at all. Or was it? So why would these shows put black men in such a weakened state, a state where a petite white woman can easily subdue them? Is it to make the white woman think there is no obstacle she can't overcome? No matter the size of the white woman, she can take out the big black man, the monster or serial killer; no obstacle is too great. It doesn't matter if she is trained to fight or a cheerleader; when properly motivated she will prevail. She is a white woman - hear her roar!

Or is it to show white superiority over black? If the latter, to what end? Black has given up on being superior to white; he has accepted his role as number two. Could it be just white reinforcing the pecking order of society?

The fact that in this day and time black is still being relegated as backseat riders of the American bus system of life further proves that black has yet to earn the respect of America.

Early film and television was made for people that could afford it, so black was entertainment, but now black are willing to pay and go to movies. Still, the black person in the horror movie dies, not as quickly, but seldom heroically.

In the alien car movie, the robot with the black-sounding voice dies.

When the hero is black, he can never win the day alone.

The alien attacks - the black hero leaps into action - as the chauffeur, not exactly saving the day but flying the white guy that will. In nearly every black movie or movie where there is a black actor, he is the helper. More recently black have been seen as more heroic, only it's a disguise. Black as a hero is nearly always masked by the need for white help. There will be some white person with the information or other key element that the black can't win without.

The great gripe recently is a black storm trooper. This nearly fried the Internet.

Why? Why? Why?

Certain white could not stand the thought, only to find out that he wasn't a good fighter and he worked in garbage collection - a compromise?

This trend has followed black actor from show to show, from year to year. The written word has seldom been kind to black people, so is there any wonder that black would have a difficult time trying to hold onto his passion? Every part of the entertainment industry holds black in a sort of disregard.

TV Commercial: Black and white in a car - the white guy drives. The nice house - white people live in it. When there is a non-speaking part in a movie, black gets it. Black is shown as the muscle for the villain, muscle that is used to show how strong the white hero is, as he quickly gives black a beating. The black actor is not just a personal plaything, so, too, is his persona; the blackness that movies portray when a white actor's role calls him to be tough, with a black jacket and dark hair. The good guy in cowboy movies wore a white hat. The bad guy wore black. The entertainment industry is definitely keeping black and white opinions of each other as their own personal race baiter toy (intentional?).

With movies and television as a constant stream of information, the way white view black is understandable. The only question is why don't entertainers and entertainment companies change?

The way black view white is with fear and an uneasy respect. The fear comes from seeing white in movies and matching those movies with white deeds. A black man was dragged behind a truck until his head came off. This happened not in the slave days or Jim Crow era, but in the twentieth century (not that this barbarism didn't happen in those earlier times). A prominent football player killed some dogs, and the white world came to the dog's defense, and to this day some have not seen fit to forgive and forget nor have they used their money to shut down animal shelter that kills every day.

Black has not yet earned the respect of America. How is black still the black child that white brought from across the ocean? Is it because white need to be superior? Is it that simple? The black actor of the past would kill to be the butt of jokes, of the black actor of now. The black actor is still shown little respect, but the money is good. The roles are better; there are more chances for black to be in charge. The black actor cannot only have a say as to how the movie goes, but how the money goes.

As with everything American, it is evolving, so what is the holdup as it relates to black actors getting more? As much as it seems racial, maybe it is just economical. In the beginning it was who had the money to spend; now it is who will spend, and on what will they spend? Again, black is his own worst enemy. The fact that black has grown an "I'm not giving money to what I can get for free" attitude gives white all the more reason to forget them. While sneaking into a movie, buying bootleg movie and music equals less coverage for blacks; they all sing the same song - white folks do the same thing. Right?

The same thing:

"What's wrong, top sergeant?

"I got trouble - the worst kind of trouble, white woman trouble!"

(passage from *Sergeant Rutledge* movie)

The same thing: As early black learned, there is no such thing as the *same thing* when it comes to black and white.

White wrong and black error is the same. Black error and white mistake are grounds for black losing a $100 million contract. Black indiscretion is grounds for losing a massive amount of endorsement. White will and have always held black to a higher standard, a standard that white doesn't aspire to. White has no need to aspire to the standard they set for black, why should they? The leader leads and the followers follow. White has preached, "Do as I say, not as I do" from the dawn of American life. The same relates to white misdeeds; they are never comparable to the misdeeds of black.

The standard that white has given to black dates back to the slave rule:

"Learn quick, work hard, and make me money."

When black is on the big and small screen, he is there to make money for white, so if he is killed, white will avenge him; if he is the villain, white will kill him. If he is the muscle, white woman will kill him, not only for racial reasons, but for financial ones as well. When television makes money, it comes from advertising, and it is difficult to have white buy $100 jeans from some white actor that is second to black. Television and movies have racial motives; some are aimed at black, but most are aimed at the white dollar.

Keeping black in a tightly controlled box is as much of a byproduct as it is racial.

Maybe?

Through wars and wealth, white built America into a superpower, not American white. The tools that they used, were and are still considered tools: black bodies, steel, and lead. The government and the people are tools also, and America is the living body.

White feeds her with well-meaning jests and halfhearted tears. America in the mind of white is what everyone should bleed. The fact that white has used America the ideal to line their pocket is no different than using black backs and blood to build America. So, it is to America that black must learn to pay respect to, but how? The same way that white has - the law, the land, and removable respect, a respect level that fluctuates and is only used when power is needed and tempered when power is gained.

Respecting the promise that care will be taken when matters of the voters comes up, after power is gain - stalling takes place of respect.

In the movies when a Latino is in a relationship with white, their skin is lightened; if the relationship is with black, the skin is darkened. The removable respect is in place. A male or female actor respects their craft, but their skin is something else, a removable respect. In the 1960s the Negro was an up-and-coming man of America. He was a husband with all the faults and shortcomings a man could have, but he was seen as a man. He was a man that had to be put in a place where white could control him, somewhat.

He was viewed as someone that could someday overtake some whites in the pecking order of America. This thought causes some white to take matters into their own hands. This action causes other whites to disassociate themselves from what they viewed as the pot calling the kettle black. Civilized as America wanted to seem, television showed the world that this was not the case.

In the 1960s, the Negro woman was an up-and-coming mother with all the shortcomings of a woman. She was upwardly mobile - she was using all of her to get and stay where she chose to go.

In the 1960s, the Negroes were coming into their own. They knew what they wanted, and they used white to get it. In the 60s they finally had enough schooling to give enough of them an adequate education, an education that not only taught them America rule, but also American manipulations, how to circumvent the system and the people, how to fight with the hands of the enemy, how to fight without fighting, how to use what American used to become a superpower, other people.

The 60s Negro was becoming comfortable with his black skin and his blackness. He was becoming American. Four deaths later, and nearly all was lost.

The upwardly mobile Negro became black skin. Schools became institutions of confinement. Family became live-in strangers. Men became sperm donors, women - factories of care - care for a child, care for the man, and care for herself, maybe? The Negro became people acting black. The massive disappearance of black men sent black boys to street school, only to grow up incomplete, adult but seldom men, able to produce children only ignorant as to how to parent them. The massive disappearance of black men sent black girls to look for black care, the care that they should have gotten from black fathers – but instead got from men, some black, some not, nearly all incomplete. She would become an adult but incomplete, able to produce children but ignorant as to how to keep the father in the life of them both.

The Negro became the producer of crime. The young black man without guidance learns that death is easier than living, killing is easier than trying. Prison is better than uncertainty; love is for suckers.

The young black woman is allowed to procreate with the knowledge of the child's future in doubt - doubt of a child's future is the fear of all parents, but black doubt is more visible. All that black is, good and bad, can in most cases be tied to white.

Chapter 9:

White Power

Human life on this planet comes from one of three places; an all-powerful GOD, aliens, or a pool of cosmic soup in Africa. The *where* is as complex as the *why*.

The outcome is that whatever the source, white skin is winning the race to the top.

Whatever or wherever the top is, how life starts, if success in life is the race, then the race originated in Africa. Black skin starts the race with all beings as equal as we are now, equal or as equal as we were ever going to be. Africa was the starting line, and Africa is where white left his blackness. The white family tree is transplanted in Europe, with branches extending to America and the Western Hemisphere.

When humans left Africa to populate the rest of the world, they started to fade from black; white not only faded its skin, but its black mind. With constant reincarnation, weather changes and war, white faded his blackness to the point that when he came back to Africa he could not recognize the black body that he had left in the wilds of that continent.

The beginning of white power starts and ends with war. White can be readily recognized as descendants of barbarians, or descendants of people they chose to call barbarians. People like the Goths, Gauls, Mongols, Huns, Vandals, and Vikings, barbarians that will go on to become the Russian, German, French, Spanish, and all other ethnicities and races that make up and has made up Europe, the Middle East, and Asia. From Africa and caves, white built the three empires that established the world civilizations: Egypt, Italy, and Greece. Every white race can trace its beginning to these three regions. Whites can also trace their lust for power to these three empires. White can trace their white power back to these three places. Egypt, for all its great wonder, launches white on their way to the top. Though some will point to hieroglyphs of Egyptians with brown skin, this is or was only a temporary stage of workmanship and evolution, a stage not unlike every incarnation of white. The brown will soon fade to resemble the white-like skin of today. The fade will also pull Egyptians away from the brown thinking of their ancient ancestors. To have had brown skin, people did little to keep the brown in modern-day Egypt. Little effort was made to keep a brown way of thinking in Egypt. Black evolution was not maintained. Egypt was prevented from becoming a placeholder in world history. Egypt was conquered by the Greeks and

Romans, and Rome conquered the known world with black and brown in their place, Roman as the leader with black and brown helpers.

The accolades of conquest are and have been short-lived - to be on top with no thought as to who was on the bottom – led to disaster. It took time for the concept of war to be misused by the offspring of the empire builders of Rome, but it happened. Yet, the conquest of the Romans was not just conquest; it was an example. It was to show America how to be or how not to be.

White in the Bible teaches white how to be and how not to be; white in the Bible is moral and immoral; white in war is both hero and villain. The Bible will show white versus all other shades of brown, and in the end, white will prevail. In ancient history, white was the hero, villain, and savior. Whites will write and rewrite their history and the history of the vanquished. Egyptians built the great pyramids, though the *why* and *how* has been lost to the ages. The Romans built the great Coliseum, and the *how* and *why* are known, at least somewhat known. These architectural splendors were built with slaves to entertain the powerful and the masses. The Greeks built the pantheon that was a showplace then as now, but this, too, was a teaching tool to America. The Gauls who would later become the French brought terror to Rome, and in turn made Rome strong. The battle of fear and overwhelming power made the Romans fight harder. The fact that they fought through their terror is what made them Roman. The European white set the table for American white to eat from. The Mongols and the Huns gave Asia a foothold in their future countries. Genghis Khan and Attila the Hun showed European whites what battle could be without rules. White became a willing student to all manner of war and the outcomes of war. War between European white, Mongols, and Huns will only make American white stronger. While European white was developing tactics for war, they were in effect designing a blueprint for America that was to be.

American white will learn all aspects of warfare. American white will do to war what the Mongol and Huns did for death - turn it into art. Americans will fight the good fight and allow the world to heap praise onto her prideful shoulders.

In fourteen hundred and ninety-two, Columbus sailed the ocean blue. He got lost, and he and his men killed thousands of natives in South America and the Caribbean. Still, he is celebrated in the country that he may or may not have discovered, a place that already was home to people that did discover it. At the World Fair, Senator Chauncey M. Depew gave this speech:

44 authentic portraits of him have descended to us, and no two of them are counterfeits of the same person…strength and weakness, intellectuality and stupidity, high moral purpose and brutal ferocity, purity and licentiousness, the dreamer and the miser, the pirate and the puritan are the types from which we may select our hero; we dismiss the painter and piercing with the clarified vision of the dawn of the 20th century the veil of 400 years we construct our Columbus.

These are the adjectives that describe America, and in no small part, Americans. From the dawn of biblical time to the landing of the pilgrim on Plymouth Rock, America has had a destiny; its ending has yet to be written, but America's beginning is legendary. The early settlers were saved from death by strange people, only to later take their saviors' land.

The early settlers brought with them a thirst for the New World and everything the native people had to offer. The thirst turned to greed, and the newcomers became outwardly hostile in their actions. This hostility eventually subsided, and peace would prevail between the two combatants, but only after early whites got all that they want.

Part of what they wanted was to turn the natives into versions of themselves. White America forced the native children to dress and speak as they saw fit.

White power.

As adults, at least some of them would want this for their children, and some adults would want it for themselves. Natives were the first of many to fall under the spell of white skin and white power. Natives became proud to call themselves *Indian*. They fought other Native people for the privilege of being called *friend* by white. Like the Native people centuries earlier, others would fall under the spell of white power. Asians would have eye surgery to round their eyes; all manner of races will fear the given name of their father. They readily surrendered the culture and identity of their last name to move closer to or at least not be pushed away from American white.

White power.

But unlike black slaves, the native people would fight and die in a struggle they could not win.

What native people were not aware of was that white had been on a full-scale war march from the beginning of civilized time. Native war was not on the same scale when it came to the war experience of their opponent. The Native war was over before it started. The war fought by Native people only served to shine a light on the weakness of black, as viewed by white. An unwinnable war fought to the death led white to respect the warrior even while disrespecting all treaties the two races had made.

White power.

What would have happened if the natives had simply allowed the first European arrivals to die?

By the time the first arrival came to what is now called America, white had discovered that the world was not flat; a death or a hundred was not going to stop others from coming. The side effect of centuries of travel and war had made white virtually unstoppable when it came to going. With war conquest, white earned not only the respect of one warrior to another, but also the respect of impersonation.

To mimic someone is said to be the sincerest form of flattery. Then whites should sincerely be flattered. They took land from an indigenous people, forced these people into slave labor, and made them sick, and still the conquered wanted to be more white-like.

The student became the teacher. Leaving the protection of British rule, the early white became manifest of its own destiny. The upstart battled the more experienced parent, but used methods learned from an early opponent. With the help and knowledge of natives, early white became American:

White power.

With dignity and pride intact, America began to conquer the world - one movie, one television show, one fashion trend at a time, with a little war in between. From emperor Augustus to George Washington, white has made a living out of turning enemies to friends, all the while waging war after war. In the time of the great Roman Empire, Rome made being a Roman the only and best thing to be. The heyday of the motion picture movie made *Coming to America* the goal to want.

White power.

Now, being American today is what being Roman was in the first century. With television and movies, people of the world are carving themselves up to be more American-like. Even people that claim America is a corrupt country only pay homage to America the beautiful. Their poisonous word only makes the rest of the world take note of the influence that America has on the world.

White power.

From Roman battles America learned; from Roman missteps American learned. The lesson that America learned came from a desire to appear different. This America was to be different, only it became rich and powerful first. The rich and powerful are different from a written point of view. The rich and powerful are different from the approach of *who can become rich and powerful*. This America is the same as ancient Rome; it sometime tries to control the reins of power and wealth. This America is still growing in its efforts to be united. This America is still ruled by white. White in America faded its black skin, but more importantly, it faded its black mind.

The black mind was sometimes duped into getting caught by slave catchers, and at other times simply gave in. White faded his black mind in the sense that he could not only enslave another person, but also rape and torture and profess to care - all in the same breath.

White power.

White faded his black mind to fear, his journey across open ocean; hostile and inhospitable land assisted in his rise to power. This is what white needed black to see - their white struggle to get to the top of America. Black often sees only the slave side of America. They don't understand that the white struggle was as strenuous as the slave struggle, just with a different outcome and different skin. Black people do not truly understand white history.

White history is a history of war. When black left Africa, white began to fight; venturing into the unknown was his first battle; learning to live off the land of the unknown was the second battle. Learning to keep others from taking from him was third, and finally came the battle to rid himself of an African way of thinking.

Every other battle is an offshoot of these four. White did all of this with a primitive brain. The primal white crossed vast land masses. Be it desert, jungle, or open water, white made a way out of no way. When some could go no further, others went farther. The one that stayed learned the land and made it home. Not only did they live but they thrived - they turned rivers into farms, wolves into man's best friend, and animals of the land into livestock. White contributions to this planet are immeasurable; the things he has tried is a library unto itself.

White power.

White buildings emerged from time gone by and still dot the landscapes of today. Black reading about these things does little to bring into focus what white has done. These great accomplishments were achieved by early man and all of his incarnations.

Then later Egyptians, Greeks, and Romans, Arabs and Asians showed the world what could be done and what will be done. After the fall and subsequent failure of these great civilizations, Britain became the superpower. The Saxons rose up out of the shadow of the great empire to lead the world in the ways of European tradition, a tradition that would fail them as it related to the New World Order to come.

With years of fighting, Britain was little different than the empires that came before it, with one very big difference: Religion. With wealth and knowledge, the whole of Europe was in flux; the old ways were waning. The rules of the church were constricting, and some wanted out. Enter the Puritans, and with them the Pilgrims, and they embarked on the trip that would reunite black and white.

White power.

As Puritan and Pilgrim fought over how the new land should be governed, they failed to understand the pain that came with starting a new anything, but as with all things white, there was something guiding - waiting to help them on their way. The first people on what would later become America left the newcomers to themselves at first, only to help them when they really needed it. With a spark from the natives and fuel from across the ocean the new world was set ablaze. Riches were squeezed out of the east coast that fed the master across the ocean. As riches came out of the new world, more visitors came to see for themselves - and few left.

One boatload became thirteen colonies, and they will in short order not be beholden to anyone.

White power.

The sons and daughters of Neanderthals, Cro-Magnons, Homo-Sapiens, Greeks, Romans, and European citizens were on the stage, and they would show the world the error that their predecessors had made. They would use black as no other had done before or has done since. They will use their king as no other had done; they will make a country as different as it will be like all others.

They will carve a superpower out of the soul of Europe. After five years of battle the thirteen colonies became a nation, and white used black, native, and French to beat back the most powerful army at the time. Some black were freed, others not, by design or not.

White had made black think that with a little luck the American dream could one day be theirs, and this kept black fighting.

White power.

While the new nation was coming into its own, so, too, were American whites, and they were in no mood to share.

White power.

In 1838, the ground wept with the dead and dying of the Native people that had fought and died - learned and was taught that white was a force to be reckoned with, and the price for the lesson was to give up all they had to white, and in turn they would be allowed to live in controlled freedom.

White power.

The Cherokee in the East was forced to move west, and it was not by some unnamed bureaucrat pushing paper; the trail of tears was put forth by no less than the president of America.

White power.

Not that it was by war; at this point war wasn't something the Native wanted with America. The Native went through what they considered was the route to go - they went through the court because America was a country that had laws and lived by them. Only the laws were for America to use at her leisure, and Native had done all the pleasing America needed. America the free had shown her color, and the color was white. The court was attempting to live by the code that America had told herself and the world that she was going to live by, but America is only the body - a body made up of oftentimes uncompromising parts, and Andrew Jackson was in no mood to hear or be told how to deal with non-white native people.

White power.

Not only did white America not want free black, they did not want a strong Native population, and they did not want to share the wealth that America had hidden in the hills and foothills of the lands and streams.

All that would come to America got the "you don't belong here" treatment, all while white was claiming the natives' land for themselves, simultaneously shrinking the native footprint and building them a prison made of the land itself. German and Irish and other Europeans "did not belong," but stayed and prospered.

Immigrants prospered while Natives suffered - why? The immigrants had at least four things going for them:

1. Knowledge: they had European knowledge, and that knowledge mirrored the knowledge of America.

2. The same customs and courtesies.

3. The same drive and thirst for things and freedom.

4. Kinship through bloodlines and ethnic connections.

America was growing so fast that there were places for everyone that came; you only had to stake out a place and hold on long enough for others to pass you by. Then you wrote back home to get more of the people that spoke your language. They became the family that your family could interact with, marry into, and help protect from the natives attack that would only backfire on the Native people, a backlash that would echo across America and bring untold pain on Native people perpetrators and non-perpetrator alike.

Religion: the immigrant worshipped in a manner that American whites could recognize, even if they did not agree with it. It was not the mumbo-jumbo of the native people, and it was not black voodoo. It was what white had seen and learned.

White power.

No matter the backlash, white was still white. It was easy to dismiss the language, easy to say *go home*, easy to say *you don't belong*, but with an attack on white skin, they banded together as they had done in the brutal earlier centuries. It was seldom if ever that white would allow other white to be dealt with harshly. That was a task held for other white. The fact that American white did not want other white in America did not mean that other white wasn't helpful, because the one thing white skin brings is drive. The drive to be: to be better, to be successful, to be first, to be unique among other white. American white was so gifted at being white they often used other Natives to do the work of keeping their kin in line.

White power.

Manifest Destiny - or war - as it became known to Mexico.

President Polk in his zeal to put his stamp beside that of the other leaders of America wanted to add to the size of America, so Mexico needed to be militarily persuaded to shrink the size of their country so America could increase its size.

It needed to be done, so in the American spirit it was done. War with Mexico. In 1848 Mexico got smaller and with, "a God-given right" America got larger and richer. Gold in the West, slaves and cotton in the South, industries in the Northeast, and war on the horizon, America was pushing and pulling herself forward, and dragging black along for company and work. The America dream was awakened in the soul of white; the ability to build a country was a chance to show the world what freedom and understanding could look like. It was also the chance to mold minds and shape thinking. America was a dreamer's paradise; with hard work and determination a man could build himself a legacy, something that would last for eternity. The problem was there were a lot of men, and they all wanted to be right, and they were all white - they wanted to be heard.

Civil war: a war between different factions of the same nation, this is the definition. What happened in America was war, and white was seldom civil about the way they waged war.

The War Between the States showed the world that America was different. They were as cordial as they were cantankerous. They were as giving as they were thieves. They were as warm as they were cold. The whites in America were as conflicted as they were conceited, the thing that still plagues them today.

When the Pilgrims landed in the land that would become America, they came with white arrogance, a sense that no matter the plight, *we shall prevail*. No matter the struggle, *we will persevere*. White came to America the land, and infected it with their arrogance; it was as if the very air they breathed was intoxicated with it.

White was seen to be better than all others, and American white was the cream of the crop.

White power.

Where does this arrogance come from? War. This is what black does not understand. He cannot get his mind to comprehend the pride that centuries of war have given to white. He cannot understand that white sees him as the weak that wants to share in the spoil of war without having skin in the battle. The end of World War Two brought black into America as paper equals. What black learned in the Great War, he took home to start using as paper equality and his black pride. White only saw and continues to see how they built America. They have little need for acknowledging the contributions of the tools they used, and black was and will continue to be thought of as only one of many tools that white uses to carve America out of the hand of an "inferior" landholder.

Black would not be placed on the back burner as before. White will deal with him, but only if he can stay strong. Whether or not white knew that black wouldn't stay strong is not known, but just in case black could stay strong, white placed hurdles in their path: drugs and a steady stream of hurt from white meant black would weaken.

During and after World War Two, moving pictures flicker, and the world saw how good it was to be an American. The feats of war heroes sprang to life on the screen; white was as always the hero and the villain, the one that caused great tragedy and the one that saved the masses from certain death. White not wanting to fight in Europe, for Europe only, gave credence to the civility that was streaming through America or the movie version of civility in America, when the Japanese bombed Pearl Harbor, America was forced into a war that most did not want to be involved in just days earlier, but others reveled at the chance to show the fortitude of America from the very beginning. The ones that hesitated to go to war showed the world the two faces of America: the America that was not a bloodthirsty country bent on conquering the world, and the one that was willing to fight the good and just fight.

The Japanese only saw the passive face, and with that as the backdrop the Japanese thought America had no stomach for the fight.

Wrong.

Not only did America have the will to fight, but she also had the cunning to play the public at home and abroad. The cunning made an enemy a friend, and a friend to fight all, including each other, while America gained the upper hand on both. The picture of heroic general and dog face soldier fighting the good fight endeared the world to America.

The horrible picture of Jews in concentration camps melted the heart of white, giving them the fire to fight to the finish wherever the finish line was.

Being passive-leaning made America look as if for the first time in recorded history a superpower was willing to keep only what it had. America did not make herself a superpower; she allowed the name to be given. The rest of the world created empires to themselves; America was an empire unto herself, and that was the way she wanted it. The fact that America acted in such a selfless manner gave the world the impression that she could be trusted to be fair and humble, and she could, just not as it related to people of color - Native, Asian and Mexican; red, yellow, and brown. All were looking for what they could not find in their country of origin. All were treated in a manner consistence with the treatment of black, but unlike black, other newcomers all had something black did not have: a country.

The hyphenated American is the only thing that keeps black in close proximity to white. Hyphenated American all has some unspoken allegiance to somewhere else. Internment camps: while Japanese-Americans were fighting in World War Two, their families were confined to internment camps; they were imprisoned because of who they could be, not who they were. When they wanted to fight, they fought. They fought their countrymen all while fighting to be accepted as American.

White power.

Some Mexican-Americans have descendants lived in three different countries, all while never moving - France, Spain, and America, still most would rather be American than any other incarnation. The Mexican-American, with all the mistreatment at the hand of white, still would rather be white than Mexican, and they would rather be Mexican than black or black-like or thought to be black-like. They were even willing to go to court to fight the black designation. No matter the indignities placed on people of color by white; white is still the life all or nearly all strived to be more like.

White power.

White gained power at the tip of a blade, and has only changed the blade. They have waged war more successfully than any other race on the planet. Race relations in America is just that - a relation; it is two group trying to be one. America is too complex for it to happen, so it never will. There will never be a black-white relationship, at least not if black is the pursuer.

Dr. King wanted his children to be judged by the content of their character, not the color of their skin. Little did he know that the great-grandparents that marched and went to jail with him would be pushed aside and become helpless in directing the character of the black child. Little did he know that drugs would crowd out his dream for black people. People that he gave his soul to, the soul black allowed to become infested with apathy. Dr. King did not understand that while he was fighting the fight, that Gandhi showed the world could be successful. There were two errors in his judgment.

One: the Mahatma was fighting non-violence in his own country, not a country he was trying to belong to.

Two: white admire and respect the fight, although his non-violence was fight without fighting, and it was short-lived. White was more afraid of Malcolm X than losing money with another march. While they wanted and were willing to compromise for money, the fact that Malcolm X was on the other side of the equation made white weigh its option. The best and quick answer was death.

White power.

If black wanted equality he would have to earn it, and not off the black of his black ancestors - nor trading off the skin of the veteran of the past. Black will have to make his own way.

White power.

Chapter 10:

Tough Love and Hard Times

Where are race relations in America headed?

To understand where we're going as a society, race relations must be defined, and the closest definition is father-son and brother-sister.

The father-son aspect:

A white senior looks across America and sees black and white. When the father sees his sons doing well, he swells with pride - how white felt about Tiger Woods and Michael Vick.

When white sees his sons falter, white takes this as the ultimate betrayal, such as with Michael Vick and Tiger Wood.

Why?

White knows the mistreatment that was inflicted on black, so to see blacks rise from nothing to achieving success despite their struggle, this gives white a calmness that allows white to be at peace with the black-white relationship. Whites then feel that their unjustness wasn't too severe.

So to watch black fall from such a height is to see the child that failed; white calm turns to mild anger; whites see their failure in every failed black life.

When the black-white relationship changes, it's at the young end. The young white-black relationship is different than the senior white relationship.

The senior white see the white-black relationship from a father-son perch. Young white has seen the black-white relationship as brother to brothers, such as with sports and war. As brothers, white can beat black and black can beat white, but no one else can fight either. As brothers, the relationship shifts from brotherly rivalry to white-black rivalry, and back again, while constantly thinking of each other as brothers.

Senior white still thinks in terms of father-son, only the father sees his son differently.

As a father, white is conflicted - he wants both of his sons to do well, but he knows that there are times he has to help one by denying the other. There will be times when the father will allow his black son to shine. Black shine is mostly what is best for the father, or what is best for wealth: think sports. White will push out his white sons to bring black in for sports' sake. More often it is black that is denied the opportunity to shine.

Then there are those times when black shines in spite of white. This is when all the slavery rhetoric bubbles to the surface - think President Obama.

It is difficult for senior white to see his white son falling behind while having every opportunity to succeed. It is difficult to see black achieve while putting forth efforts to hamper black progress. To use the father-son, brother-sister analogy (which black or white doesn't), then and only then can race relations move forward.

Blacks must understand where whites came from and how whites think of blacks. White come from power and they see black as coming from weakness. Some black amplifies this thinking by their claiming they are grateful that slavery freed them from Africa. Some black amplifies this thinking by begging white store to take black money, other force their way into white life, housing, country clubs. White can view these intrusion as a pet needing the cress of their master. Black constant need to be white like and to be like by white only keep black wanting.

Whites must understand their power - the power they wield and the power they project. Often it is the latter that forces black to think dark black. White must understand that slavery wasn't a problem for black 40 acre and a mule was, the hope, the thought of compensation. Busing was a problem, integration was a problem. Desegregation was a problem. Integration was a problem for black and desegregation was a problem for white. Forcing white to interact with black only make black weaker and more hated. Slavery in degrees wasn't a problem, lynching was a problem, beating was a problem, rape was a problem and these crimes wasn't slavery. These crimes and the perpetrator are and has been the problem. It was not only a problem for black it was and is a problem for the individual. Black understanding of this treatment means different thing to the individual, work harder, give in, fear, hate...

"pull yourself up by your own boot strap" White way of saying they are not responsible for the masses. Black has tried with mix success; black wall street, black crime, black politician all had and have certain levels of failure that are white in nature. White must understand that black isn't their problem the problem with the minority white is rich white. Whether black is here or Africa white money is still going to be white money. The boots strap analogy will still be used. There are crime and class system in homogenous country.

Black men are more likely to be incarcerated than go to college. All have heard the stats, the dire warnings, and all have moved on, hoping that their offspring will be the few that will achieve success. For many, the cost of black success will be the price of blackness itself. The fade of blackness can be seen every day in reality television, any sporting event, or any school bus stop.

For reality TV to survive it needs ratings; to get ratings there must be controversy. White controversy it understood. Black controversy is the weak, shining a spotlight on the weakness of a race, the catch-22 of fame. Act weak, act the buffoon, get the wealth. The money makes the weakling strong, the buffoon wise, but it can cripple the race as a whole.

Does the end justify the means?

Yes, but only for the drop, not the ripple.

If white is the cause of black strength and weakness, then white must either strengthen all or care for the weak.

Why?

The prime directive: the creator of Star Trek, Gene Roddenberry, knew (or the writer knew) that if the Enterprise interfered with the natural evolution of a species, you could force the species to grow beyond their understanding. The slave trade did just what Gene Roddenberry did not want to do to fictional aliens. When black was in Africa, he was in a slow evolutionary growth cycle; there was little need for weapons that could not be thrown or wielded by hand. There was little need for farming beyond the boundary of a hut.

There was no need to build monuments to God, leaders, or self. The growth cycle was slow because the need was small. Forced evolution caused by the slave trade accelerated black physical evolution, while the black mental state lagged behind naturally and by white power. The mixing of DNA also expedited the physical and mental growth of black. The mental effect of mixing DNA forced black to separate from other black. The mixing of DNA allowed certain blacks' mental state to keep up with his or her physical evolution.

In the early years, the mixing of DNA kept the slave bewildered; the skin color, his homeland, and his countrymen put everything that was going on in his brain at odds with his eyes. He could think like no other before him, he could reason, but his thinking and reasoning kept bringing him to the same conclusion.

Why?

Why is black skin treated this way, while white skin is treated that way? Why do whites preach one thing then do another?

Why?

The answer can only come from whites, but there is no way for them to truly know or understand the question. White people don't dislike Black people; white people dislike the black persona they created: the fictional black man, the one that wants to rape all white women, the fictional black man that can't be killed with just one bullet. The fictional black man that can't be educated. The fictional black woman that is not harmed by rape like a white woman would be. The fictional black teen that is angry and will grow up to be angrier and more dangerous. The fictional black people that whites put in movies and on the television screen - these are the black people that whites dislike.

But with the prison population being what it is, there has to be a real version of these types of black people, right?

Yes, there are, and white created them. In most cases whites didn't physically turn blacks into rapists, murderers, and criminals; no, whites just did what they wanted to and black thought they would do the same. White made their life look so great that it destroyed the identity of anyone that looked at white for too long.

The "war on Islam" is the perfect example. Extremists have convinced themselves that America is the great Satan, not understanding that it is really themselves that are corrupting the minds of their children. They have looked into white life too long, and they have started to destroy themselves from the inside. Like many before them, they are fighting a color – a color that has them surrounded, a color that has waged war on every continent in every form. The extremists miss the irony that they are now begging whites to join the fight with them, and some whites will.

The greatest threat to America and to Islam is at some point in time white will join the extremists. At several point in the history of rap, white has been the highest paid rapper, white was the last samurai (even if it was just a movie), white has influenced many tribes and countries, and many have looked too long at white life and found that they love it - love it to the point where they sold and gave away family secrets.

More books have been written by whites about other races than other races have read. In short, white people know how to be white and how to fight better than any other race fights, while other races only know how to emulate white or hate white for being who they have always been. Extremists are begging white to join their fight; what they, like all the others before them don't understand, is that whites don't follow. They lead and will lead if given the opportunity. They will remake extremism into their own whiteness. The war that the extremists are fighting has no ending. Their fight has no real attainable goal. They well never rule the world. Their message can't conquer their followers.

Black fought for the right to maybe one day be free. Black fought with less than other soldiers. Black fought with less respect than the respect given to the enemy. Black still idolized white. Black still wants to be white-like. Extremists are crippling their religion and their children for the right to die for a cause that is unattainable, a cause that has not been attained in 2,ooo years. Religion and racial purity have failed in every century since the dawn of time. The death toll is only making whites richer; the destruction is only making Islam weaker. Death for the sake of death is white fighting without fighting. Hating America is not the same as hating white, killing Americans is not the same as killing white, fighting America is not the same as fighting white. White is the color - America is the idea.

If black people want the equality they say they want, then they have to make themselves attractive to white people. Black people have to vote as a block. They have to, in effect, go back to being the black folk of the 1950's and 1960's. They have to get back to not only knowing "thy neighbor" but also helping "thy neighbor." Blacks must start to hold their children accountable and buy them only what they earn. They must hold men accountable to their wives, girlfriends, and children. Women must learn that sometimes more is best and less gets you less until you are used to less.

Do black lives matter? With the rash of police shootings, blacks are in crisis mode - protesting, marching, yelling that black lives matter, but do they mean it?

The short answer is no. Black lives don't matter, not to white and not to black. Black death matters. While blacks are marching and protesting, their children are the worst in education, black life. Their children are the worst in job retention, black life. But their children are tops in over- spending on clothes and shoes, tops in being correctly imprisoned, tops in killing other kids (not in mass killing). Black lives haven't mattered to black since the crack era. The police taking of black lives matters, but the outrage is somewhat hypocritical. When blacks are not outraged when it happens to black on black, when blacks are not outraged when it happens to other races. When black can only tell white what they should do, without saying what black is going to do, then white just waits for the false sincerity to die out and allow things to proceed as always.

Like the extremist, black has allowed white to give a shadow understanding. The shadow is dark with no depth. Black think that they deserve equal treatment from white but that is not true; dark thinking has no depth.

Why should white treat black as an equal? Black has little to offer anyone. Black women that make porn earn less than white women. White actors that look mixed race make more money than a black actor. With Indians from India looking black and sounding white, there is little need for American black skin. Blacks have nowhere to go; they are stuck with the treatment they get.

Now, should black be treated as an equal? Yes, but *should* doesn't mean *deserve*. In order to get the equality that blacks say they want, they must make themselves attractive to white.

How? Money: save more, spend less. Acquire more; stop demanding to be let into the white world. Stop forcing white to take black money. Vote, all for one, just maybe not all the time. Follow the history that white required you to learn. Get an ally. White has ruled the world from the comfort of America by having allies. Even the allies that don't trust America will bend a little to her will. Black needs an ally, some race that will allow them to look better to the date that brought them to the dance.

Education. Black was famous for the discipline they bestowed on their children. Now black gives excuses to explain failure:

"There are no jobs here."

"Move."

"Why should I have to move?"

"There are no jobs."

"If they would bring some jobs we would not have to move."

"What about picking vegetables?"

"I ain't doing that."

"Do you have any skills?"

"Typing, building."

"Is there something you can do that not everyone can do?"

If there is no work, there is no work. Hispanics have shown that in a lot of cases jobs are available, just not the type that blacks will do. Why? Again, white power white have made certain feel distasteful to the black mind. The thought of working in the field again give black slave vision. Vision that black under 60 should have. Black under 60 know very little about slavery, still certain job black will not do not consider. Black will wallow in poverty be for saying I work in the field for a white man (some anyway).

White people have to understand that there is a reckoning coming, and it may not be black, but it will be a non-white, and the only opportunity to stay mildly influential is to build a bridge. The best bridge is acknowledgement, to acknowledge the might and misdeeds of the mighty, to be more inclusive, less confrontational. The world needs to understand that America is not golden, it's brass, it will tarnish, and it will be in need of constant polishing.

America is not as united as she can be, not as stately as she wants to be, but America will shine and America will be what everyone needs it to be, whenever they need her to be. The race relations in America are the same as America herself - never golden, only brass always in need of a touch-up, and like America you must look underneath to find how race works and destroys. Unlike America, race is not an idea; race is real people with real concerns and a real need to talk and talk and fight and cry and accept the fact that some things are unchangeable; slaves were slave; black skin does identify a black criminal, not a black race. White has stereotyped black to the point that they have created their own demon - the demon will have his rights violated. The demon that white created must understand that screaming and demanding will get you shot. Your family will enjoy the victory over the shooter and the white populace, but you will be dead.

Yes, blacks have rights. Those rights are not comforting the children of the dead. Whites have in no uncertain terms shown their contempt and bias toward black skin. They have for centuries killed and gotten away with the killing of all races. Black can't expect white to change, black can't be shocked that they can provoke white and run from white. They can't give white a reason to be white. White rule can only be broken by new rules and rulers. Education and voter participation will change the rule and the ruler, if we want them to change, or we as black skin can allow the loudest and the nastiest of white skin to silence the other skin people and in effect ourselves.

White skin is allowing Old World thinking to influence their thinking - thinking that has been shown to be unattainable and unsustainable. White skin is cutting off its nose to spite its face, and what could come next is what has always come next: white chaos.

.

www.ingramcontent.com/pod-product-compliance
Lightning Source LLC
Chambersburg PA
CBHW072045280526
45788CB00006B/2186